CHARLES II's MINETTE

Charles II's Minette

PRINCESS HENRIETTE-ANNE
DUCHESS OF ORLEANS

Bryan Bevan

ASCENT BOOKS
LONDON

First published 1979
by Ascent Books Ltd
Bedford Row London

Printed in Great Britain by
Butler & Tanner Ltd
Frome and London
ISBN 0 9064 0703 6

Contents

Illustrations

* *Documentations photographique de la Réunion des Musées Nationaux*

Acknowledgements

To Monsieur Martial de la Fournière, Directeur des Archives et Documentation, Ministère des Affaires Étrangères Paris and his staff for their help and courtesy during my researches. To His Excellency Sir Nicholas Henderson, British Ambassador in Paris for his interest and assistance, and to Lady Henderson for showing me the portrait of Princess Henriette-Anne, Duchess of Orleans, at the British Embassy.

To Lord and Lady Clifford of Chudleigh for their delightful hospitality at Ugbrooke, Devon and for giving me permission to study the Clifford MSS.

To His Grace the Archbishop of Canterbury for his permission to study some manuscripts in the Lambeth Palace Library and to the librarians for their assistance.

To the Director and staff of L'Institut Français in Queensberry Place for their courtesy and help in my studies. To my friend Elma Dangerfield for suggesting the idea. To my friend Desmond Seward for lending me his copy of *Oraisons Funèbres* by J. B. Bossuet and his encouragement.

To the London Library my grateful thanks for allowing me to keep essential works of reference long after the permitted period.

To Mrs. Osyth Leeston for her care and diligence in editorial work on my book.

To Sir Oliver Miller for his helpful advice concerning illustrations.

To Monsieur Hugh de Lencquesaing for his help and accompanying me to Versailles.

To the Director of the Public Record Office, Chancery Lane, for allowing me to study Princess Henrietta's original letters and the State papers of France, for their courtesy and help.

Preface

Since I wrote a short article about Princess Henrietta-Anne Duchess of Orléans for the *Contemporary Review* many years ago, I have always wanted to write a biography of the life and personality of this fascinating Stuart Princess, so beloved by her contemporaries. There is Margaret Irwin's vivid portrait of Minette in her delightful *Royal Flush* (1932), an historical novel with a strange, obsessive power. Surprisingly enough there are not many biographies on the subject. I would like especially to mention my debt to Julia Cartwright's absorbing work *Madame – A Life of Henriette, Daughter of Charles I and Duchess of Orléans (1894)*. Also to Cyril Hughes Hartmann for his massive labours and invaluable research on his book *Charles II and Madame* (1934) (not a biography). There is also the Comte de Baillon's *Henriette-Anne D'Angleterre, duchesse d'Orléans, Sa Vie et Sa Correspondance avec son frère Charles II* (1886). Madame de la Fayette's *Histoire de Madame Henriette*—by a contemporary and intimate friend of the Princess, is actually an essential work for a new biographer. Other works I have made use of are classified in my bibliography.

For my own researches I have studied all Madame's correspondence in French in the Lambeth Palace Library, and her eight letters in French among the French State Papers in the Record Office, Chancery Lane. I am familiar with almost all of her published letters in various works in the Bibliothèque Nationale in Paris. Owing to the courtesy and helpfulness of the British Embassy in Paris, and also the help of the Director of the French archives in the Quai D'Orsay I was given every facility to study the despatches of various French ambassadors preserved at the Ministère des Affaires Étrangères, Quai D'Orsay. I am grateful to them also for allowing me to study all Charles II's letters to his sister preserved in a green volume

1

Preface

(Mémoires et Documents: Angleterre Vol. 26). My only regret is that this correspondence should cease so suddenly when the preliminary negotiations for the Treaty of Dover had reached such an interesting stage. I am grateful, too, to Lord and Lady Clifford of Chudleigh for their delightful hospitality at Ugbrooke Park and for allowing me to study the Clifford MSS in their beautiful home in Chudleigh, South Devon, the former home of Sir Thomas Clifford of the Cabal, created First Lord Clifford. In Exeter is the site of Bedford House where Princess Henrietta was born in 1644, and nearby is the beautiful and historic Guildhall where the fine Sir Peter Lely hangs, presented to the City of Exeter by Charles II.

During several weeks in Paris (February 1978) through the kindness and generosity of my publishers, I was able to visit various places familiar to Madame such as Fontainebleau, Versailles and St. Cloud. I walked in the ancient Marais district of Paris as much as possible. One Sunday morning I remember particularly after a long and exhausting trudge down the Rue de Rivoli the pleasure of seeing the Hôtel de Beauvasis in the mediaeval Rue François-Miron. From there Madame and her mother Henrietta Maria watched the State Entry into Paris of the young Louis XIV and his Spanish-born Queen Marie-Thérèse. Anne of Austria's beautiful Church of Val-de-Grâce near the Boulevard de Port-Royal enchanted me. How easy it is for an author to imagine Madame accompanying her mother-in-law to this Baroque church, erected by Anne of Austria in gratitude for the birth of the infant Louis XIV in 1638. Nearby is No. 284 Rue St-Jaques where the Duchesse de la Vallière, Madame's former Maid-of-Honour, retired to become a nun after Louis XIV had tired of her in 1672. The Palais-Royal, Richelieu's Palace, Madame's home in Paris, is now the office of the Council of State. Her home in that 'palais de delices' in St. Cloud is—alas!—no more. Paris is full of memories of intimate friends of Madame, such as the Marquise de Sévigné, who lived for many years in the Hôtel Carnavalet. In the Place des Vosges, Paris's oldest Square, Marquise de

Preface

Sévigné was born and the great preacher the Abbé Bossuet also lived at No. 17.

Even after more than three centuries Princess Henrietta-Anne still has the power to make conquests of the living. The secret of her eternal fascination was her enormous charm and vivid personality. No princess was more tenderly loved by a multitude of friends, she appealed to the heart and also to the mind of those who were privileged to know her.

BRYAN BEVAN

I

'Born in the storms of War'

Of all the Princesses of the House of Stuart none was more lovable or more attractive than Princess Henrietta-Anne, youngest daughter of Charles I, later familiarly known as Madame at the Court of Louis XIV in France. Truly she belongs to both Britain and France, to Britain by pride of birth and she was never to forget that. She was a Princess of England. France, too, is deeply proud of Henriette D'Angleterre, for she was educated and passed almost all her brief life there. She was to marry Monsieur, the younger brother of the '*Roi Soleil*'. For nine vital years Madame was to play a patient, vital part, making use of her brilliant diplomatic talents in forging the links of Anglo-French friendship that culminated in the Treaty of Dover (1670).

At a critical stage of the tragic Civil War, Henrietta Maria, beloved queen of Charles I, had been compelled to say farewell for the last time to her husband on the eve of the Battle of Newbury. 'Dear Heart' as she called him in her letters. She was in acute personal danger, for she could hardly expect any mercy from the Parliamentary forces if she was captured. From Abingdon she travelled westward to Exeter where she intended to seek safety under the protection of Sir John Berkeley, Governor of Exeter, an experienced soldier and of proven loyalty to the King. It was 1 May 1644 when the Queen, who was in poor health, reached Exeter. She went at once to Bedford House, a property that belonged to the Russell family, which at that period occupied the site of Bedford Circus, between Southernhay and High Street.

Desperately anxious as he was about his wife, for he had

5

heard alarming reports about her health, King Charles immediately sent an urgent message to his chief physician in London
the Huguenot Sir Theodore Mayerne. 'Mayerne,' he wrote, 'for
love of me go to my wife—CR.' Although he was no servile
courtier, this great physician, a man with original ideas, left
for Devon with Sir Matthew Lister arriving there on 28 May.
Once when the little French-born Queen had expressed a secret
fear to Sir Theodore that she might go mad, the physician with
his rugged tongue had told her that she was already demented.
Now he was present together with Madame Peronne, the best
midwife in France, sent to her sister-in-law in her hour of trial
by Anne of Austria, the Queen-Mother of France. On 16 June
Henrietta Maria gave birth to an infant princess.

The choice of royal attendant to the delicate baby was a wise
one, for she was almost immediately entrusted to the care of
Anne Villiers, Countess of Dalkeith, who had married the elder
son of the Earl of Morton. She was related to George Villiers,
1st Duke of Buckingham, once the handsome favourite of
Charles I and of his father. Lady Dalkeith had inherited the
Villiers beauty, but she was a woman of personality, being fearless and outspoken. The Stuarts were certainly fortunate in
their devoted servants.

Robert Devereux, Third Earl of Essex, son of Queen Elizabeth I's favourite now advanced on Exeter together with the
Parliamentary forces and began to besiege the City. When
Queen Henrietta Maria applied for a safe-conduct to Bath,
Essex rudely retorted that if he escorted Henrietta Maria anywhere it would be to London to answer to Parliament for the
war. So, rather than fall into the hands of the enemy and aware
that if she did so, she would do her husband's cause irreparable
harm, the Queen decided on the desperate expedient of escaping to France. Though extremely reluctant to leave her baby
daughter, who was too young and delicate to travel, the Queen
at least had the consolation that her infant daughter was under
the devoted care of Lady Dalkeith and Sir John Berkeley.

Henrietta Maria has been charged with many faults, she was

bigoted, lacked political judgement and she was indiscreet, yet there was a certain grandeur about the little Queen, she had inherited her superb courage from her father the great Henri IV of France. The Queen managed to reach Falmouth where she embarked on a Dutch vessel. Somewhere in the Channel an English Cruiser in the Parliamentary service sighted the Queen's ship and gave chase. At this desperate juncture Henrietta Maria gave orders to the captain to blow up the ship, rather than let her fall into the hands of the enemy. A furious storm now sprang up, driving the ship on to the rocks near Brest. Well might her son Charles Prince of Wales (later Charles II), in jest with his sister sometimes allude to 'Mam's bad fortune at sea'. The Queen and her ladies were given shelter by the kindly peasants, and Queen Anne of Austria, full of solicitude, sent carriages and doctors, so that the royal fugitive could be escorted to Paris.

Meanwhile Charles I had succeeded in entering Exeter on the 26 July, having fought his way through the Parliamentary troops. It was an emotional moment for the King when he entered Bedford House where he was now to lodge, and saw for the first time his baby daughter, who had been sick with convulsions. Charles's youngest daughter was to resemble her father in physical appearance and even in character she later seemed more a Stuart than a Bourbon. She was to possess more than her share of Stuart melancholy charm, but her wit and vivacity and natural gaiety she inherited from her mother and her French forebears. Now the poor overwrought King clasped his infant daughter in his arms and thought longingly of her mother.

Charles was anxious that his daughter should be baptised according to the rites of the Church of England. There is indeed an entry in the registers of the Cathedral of Exeter showing that Dr. Lawrence Burnell, Dean of Exeter, officiated at the ceremony, and that the Sir John Berkeley, Lady Dalkeith and Lady Powlett acted as sponsors.

'Henrietta, daughter of Our Soveraigne Lord King Charles

7

and our gracious Queene Mary, was baptised the 21st of July 1644.' It was a kindly gesture of Queen Henrietta Maria's later to give her youngest daughter the additional name of Anne by way of gratitude to Queen Anne of Austria, who had been a generous friend.

Before leaving for Cornwall to continue his campaign against Lord Essex, King Charles appointed Dr. Thomas Fuller chaplain to his infant daughter. By September 1645, however, the Princess Henrietta and her governess Lady Dalkeith were in acute personal danger, for the Parliamentary generals Fairfax and Waller were once more besieging Exeter. Though Lady Dalkeith made unsuccessful attempts to escape to Cornwall with Princess Henrietta she had maintained throughout her ordeal her lion-hearted spirit. She was greatly discouraged nevertheless by the unmerited reproaches of Queen Henrietta, who was naturally watching events from France with the deepest anxiety, dreading no doubt lest her beloved baby might fall into the hands of the enemy. The royal governess at least had one influential friend Sir Edward Hyde, later Lord Clarendon, who defended the lady against the somewhat unfair criticism of the Queen.

When he appointed Dr. Thomas Fuller his daughter's chaplain, it served King Charles's purpose to demonstrate his own loyalty to the reformed church in England, for Fuller, though not bigoted avowed the Protestant faith. He was a man with many friends, among them Sir John Berkeley the governor of Exeter and Lady Poulet of Hinton St. George. Fuller was an author of considerable distinction, best known for his later great works *The History of the Worthies of England* and *The Church History of England*.

Whilst in Exeter he composed a book *Good Thoughts in Bad Times*, described by him as the first fruits of the Exeter Press.[1] He had a copy specially bound in blue morocco embellished with the Princess Henrietta's own cypher and coronet. One day when the infant princess sat in the arms of her governess Lady Dalkeith, he gave her the book. She was later to treasure this

book, and as she matured she was to develop a fastidious discriminating taste in literature. She transcribed passages in her
own hand on the title page. Yet she was too young for the
worthy Dr. Fuller to have any influence on her.

The winter of 1645 was a dramatic, stormy period in Exeter's
history, for the City was then besieged by the Parliamentary
forces. It is almost certain that the inhabitants of Exeter—a city
so loyal to the King—would have suffered starvation had not
a sudden providential flight of larks invaded the town.

Dr. Fuller wrote:
When the City of Exeter was besieged by the Parliament's
forces, so that only the south side thereof, towards the sea
was open unto it, incredible numbers of larks were found in
that open quarter, for multitude like quails in the wilderness
... they were as fat as plentiful, so that, being sold for two-
pence a dozen, and under the poor (who could have no
cheaper, as the rich no better meal), used to make pottage
of them, boiling them down therein.

Eventually on 13 April 1646 the gallant Sir John Berkeley
and the garrison were compelled to surrender, though on
honourable terms. It was imperative for Lady Dalkeith and
Princess Henrietta to move elsewhere and escorted by Sir John
Berkeley they travelled to Salisbury. Henrietta was never again
to return to her natal city, but she always retained a fondness
for loyal Exeter, and her brother Charles II referred in one of
his letters to her as 'an Exeter woman'. Visitors to the beautiful
Elizabethan Guildhall can see for themselves the portrait of the
Princess now Duchess of Orléans painted by Sir Peter Lely, presented to the City of Exeter by Charles II after her death.

Sir John Berkeley was the youngest son of Sir Maurice Berkeley of Bruton in Somersetshire, and was reputed to be descended
from Danish Kings. He is commemorated for his valour in
a tablet in Twickenham parish church.[2] He later owned

* Under this marble Lyes the renowned ashes of the Right Honourable the
Ld. John Berkeley Baron of Bruton in Somersetshire in the days of Charles

property in Twickenham Park. After the surrender, Berkeley joined his kinsman Lord Jermyn in Paris where he became a member of the household of Queen Henrietta Maria. It is probable that he had already become attached to Lady Dalkeith, for he made her an offer of marriage in France only to be rejected by the lady on the advice of Sir Edward Clarendon, the King's chief minister. Henceforward Berkeley held a lasting grudge against Clarendon.

By the terms of Sir John Berkeley's surrender the Princess and her household were permitted to travel to any place in the kingdom which her guardian might choose. Lady Dalkeith would have preferred Richmond, but the Parliamentary leaders insisted that they should go to Oatlands, the royal dower house at Walton-on-Thames, Surrey. Although Parliament had promised to provide a sum sufficient for the maintenance of the Princess and her household, Lady Dalkeith was compelled out of her own pocket to pay for the expenses of the entire household for three months. No wonder that the high-spirited lady protested vigorously in her letters to Sir Thomas Fairfax and to the speakers of both Houses. Finally an abrupt message was brought to her from the House of Commons ordering her to dismiss Princess Henrietta's household and to make arrangements that she should be escorted to St. James's Palace where she could join her sister Princess Elizabeth and brother the Duke of Gloucester. At this juncture Lady Dalkeith once again showed her independence of spirit and superb courage, for she was determined never to part with Princess Henrietta until she could safely hand her over to one or other of her royal parents.

It was only after the intrepid lady had again made courageous remonstrances to the Speakers of both Houses* and secured no satisfaction from them that she decided on more

---

I for his singular valour and conduct in recovering ye City of Exeter out of the hands of ye rebells He was made Governor thereof and one of his major generals in the West. He deceased Aug 26st 1678 in ye 72 yeare of his age.

    * Her original letter written on 28 June 1646 to the House of Lords may still be seen in the Bodleian Library.

drastic action. By this time she was convinced that the Parliamentary leaders intended to coerce her to hand over the Princess to them, so secretly and with infinite resource she decided to plan their escape to France where they could rejoin Princess Henrietta's mother.

She dared not confide the secret to members of the Princess's household except for two trusted servants named Lambert and Dyke. A French valet who was to pose as Lady Dalkeith's husband, was also entrusted with the secret. If it had not been for the lady's courage and resourcefulness, Henrietta might easily have shared the fate of her elder sister Elizabeth, who was to die when very young in the Isle of Wight, one of the Parliament's victims.

Lady Dalkeith disguised herself as a beggar woman in a shabby cloak; at the same time she artfully concealed her graceful figure by putting a hump of old rags on one shoulder. Much to the indignation of the infant princess now aged two, her governess dressed her in a ragged suit of boy's clothes, and she was given the name of Pierre.

Then lifting Henrietta on to her back, she walked all the way to Dover. The Princess even at that tender age had plenty of personality and spirit. She protested in a most vigorous way to all the passers-by on the road that she was not Pierre but the Princess and that the tattered boy's suit she was wearing was not her real suit. Fortunately nobody took her childish prattle seriously. Perhaps fifteen years later when the little girl—now Madame—was dazzling the Court of Louis XIV with the brilliance of her personality and charm, she retained some childish memory of this rare adventure.

All the way to Dover Sir John Berkeley following from a distance anxiously kept an eye on the Princess and her governess with their escort. He was greatly relieved when they boarded a French ship for Calais.

There was naturally great consternation at Oatlands when it was discovered that the Princess and Lady Dalkeith were found to be missing. The fears of the members of her household were somewhat relieved when a letter arrived from Lady Dalkeith explaining why she had been forced to take this action. Julia Cartwright in her biography of Madame Henrietta Duchess of Orleans inserts all of it.

'It will be a great mark of your faithfullness and kindness to your mistress', wrote Lady Dalkeith, 'to conceal her being gone as long as you can ... all her wearing clothes, woollen or linen, you may distribute amongst you'; Parliament did not receive intelligence of the Princess's flight for three days after her departure.

It was the preacher the Abbé Bossuet, one of France's great churchmen, who, over twenty years later in his magnificent Oraison funèbre at the funeral of Henrietta Maria, evokes this stirring episode. The words seem aflame with his eloquence:

Princess, whose future destiny is to be so great and glorious! Must you be born in the power of the enemies of your race? Eternal God! Watch over her! Holy angels, surround her with your unseen squadrons, and guard this illustrious and forsaken child. God did protect her, Messieurs! Her governess, two years afterwards, saved her precious charge from the hands of the rebels, and although conscious of her own greatness, the child revealed herself, and refusing all other names, insisted on calling herself the Princess. She was safely borne to the arms of her royal mother, to be her consolation in misfortune, and to become the happy spouse of a great prince, and the joy of all France.[2]

To call her 'the happy spouse of a great prince' must have been flattering to Monsieur her husband, but people listening enthralled to Bossuet in 1669 were well aware of her deep unhappiness.

The Princess and her governess arrived safely at Calais. Great was the joy of her mother Queen Henrietta Maria and the cavaliers in her exiled Court. When news of her daughter's safety reached her, carriages were at once despatched to Calais to transport Lady Dalkeith and her royal charge to St. Germain near Paris where the Queen was then residing.

According to her Chaplain Pere Cyprien de Gamaches, who was attached to Henrietta Maria, she regarded her daughter as *enfant de bénédiction*, and she resolved that the child with the grace of God must be instructed in the Catholic religion. It was fitting that the Princess should be brought to the Chapel of the Louvre where Pere Cyprien was her mentor.

As for Lady Dalkeith, her magnificent fortitude was praised and admired by the Cavaliers and poets at the Court of the exiled Queen. To Edmund Waller she was by 1650 'the fairest morton' for by the death of her father-in-law she had lately become Countess of Morton.

Waller, too, paid a graceful tribute to the infant princess, whose adventure had caught the imagination of her contemporaries. He wrote:

> Though now, she flies her native isle, less kind,
> Less safe for her, than either sea or wind,
> Shall, when the blossom of her beauty's shown,
> See her great brother on the British throne,
> Where peace shall smile, and no dispute arise,
> But which rules most; his sceptre or her eyes.[3]

A study of the Domestic State Papers of the Reign of Charles II provides some curious information. It contains petitions by various people, who had suffered some financial loss owing to their services to the Princess Henrietta for which they now wished some compensation. There is, for instance, the claim of Sir William Boremar, Clerk-Comptroller of the household of Charles II, during 1661 that for his services to the Princess at Exeter, he had been involved in a debt of £650. He now petitioned the King 'that he might have the keeping of the garden and groves, which he is now planting for the King's use in Greenwich Park with a fee of £100 per annum and leave to dispose of the fruit of that and other of His Majesty's gardens and orchards to his own advantage'.

It would seem that neither Elinor Dyke or Thomas Lambert prospered with the years. These were the loyal servants, who attended Princess Henrietta and her governess, on their hazardous journey to Dover and Calais. Elinor Dyke, for instance, petitions in September 1663 for arrears of wages, due to her for six years services, £25 board wages at Exeter, and £7 for silver laced shoes for Princess Henrietta, 'whom she attended into France, losing thereby her house and furniture for fifteen rooms, and now her pension of £60 is stopped, so that she has nothing left and is beholden to the Countess of Berkshire for a house to live in'.

Three years later we find Thomas Lambert and Mary his wife petitioning

for the customs of 2000 pieces of Holland linen, to enable them to drive a trade in their old age. Were obliged to save their lives by leaving the country six years for their diligence in convoying the Princess Henrietta, from her barbarous enemies to the Queen-Mother in France, are injured by searches in their millinery ware and lace for French commodities.[4]

II

Exile in France

Père Cyprien de Gamaches, who wrote a short book of *Mémoires*,[1] gives us an attractive picture of Princess Henrietta when a little girl. He tells us that the Princess of England was tenderly loved by her mother. Throughout life their relations were extremely intimate. Père Cyprien thought that fathers and mothers love with more tenderness the last children they have brought into the world, though his assertion is really open to doubt. The old father was to become deeply attached to the intelligent child: 'as soon as the first sparks of reason began to glimmer in the mind of that child', wrote Père Cyprien, 'the Queen honoured me with the command to instruct her and took the trouble herself to bring her to the Chapel of the Louvre where I taught the children Christian doctrine.' Lady Morton was always present on these occasions. One day she told the Princess laughingly: 'I think Father Cyprien's catechising is intended as much for my benefit as for that of your Royal Highness.'

Lady Morton was a Protestant, and although she may have liked the old Father, never showed the least inclination to be converted. Princess Henrietta who already revealed signs of a remarkably quick intelligence, repeated her governess's remark to her mother the Queen, who unable to resist trying to convert any possible candidate to the Roman Catholic religion, told her daughter, 'My dear child, as you are so devout yourself, why do you not try to convert your governess.'[2] Henrietta's answer—that of a lovable child—makes her very alive to us. 'Madame,' she replied, 'I do my best, I embrace her, I clasp my arms round her neck, I say to her, Do be converted, Lady

15

Morton. Father Cyprien says you must be a Catholic to be saved. Do be a Catholic, Ma Bonne Dame and I will love you still more dearly.'

Despite all their persuasions, however, Lady Morton held fast to her protestantism. When he alludes to her, Père Cyprien's references now become a little acid as if he resented her obstinacy. After her husband's death in 1651, Anne Countess of Morton obtained leave from Queen Henrietta Maria to return to England. She was never to see her Princess again, for she died three years later.

Father Cyprien relates that the Queen's elder sister the Duchess of Savoy wrote to beg her to bring up her daughter in the true faith. To satisfy the Duchess of Savoy on this point Henrietta Maria ordered the Father to publish the manual of instruction which he had drawn up for the Princess's use. This book possessed the title *Exercices d'une Ame Royale*.

When Henriette was about five, she was drawn by Claude Mellan, a French artist, who had studied in Rome and Paris. It is a very moving picture. She is wearing a simple necklace of pearls. Mellan was a lively man, full of spirit. He lived to a great age, dying from a fall he had sustained on his staircase.[3]

Queen Henrietta Maria resented passionately the criticism of the English refugees at the Court of her elder daughter Princess Mary of Orange at The Hague that she intended to make Henrietta Anne a Catholic. In those early days after the execution of her husband Charles I in 1649, she stubbornly maintained that a clause in her marriage treaty had stipulated that all the children should be brought up in her care until their thirteenth year. Her son, Charles II, tried to argue with her, then instructed the Chancellor Sir Edward Hyde to tell his mother the irreparable harm it would do his cause in England. Anyway she detested Hyde. It was all in vain. Her other children had escaped her, but her favourite child, her *enfant de bénédiction* must remain in her care and protection. All Hyde was able to obtain was a promise that Henrietta would not enter a convent.

Exile in France

It was of inestimable advantage as the Princess's later intimate friend, Madame de La Fayette observed that Henrietta was educated as a private person. She had acquired all the knowledge, the sweetness and humanity in which royal personages are too often lacking. It was fortunate for the Princess's fine character that she was thus early trained in the school of adversity.

There indeed is a resemblance between Henrietta Anne and Louise Marie the enchanting little princess born to Mary of Modena, queen of James II during their early days in exile at St. Germain (1691). Her father called her '*La consolatrice*' in the same way his mother had called her daughter *enfant de bénédiction*. Louise Marie (re-christened Louise in compliment to Louis XIV, who had been so good to the Stuarts) died too early at the age of twenty. Her brother James Francis Edward later known to the Jacobites as James III was less fortunate than Charles II, because by her untimely death he lost a great source of strength to his cause. Both princesses were educated as Catholics, and Louise Marie often went with her mother to Chaillot also familiar to Henrietta whose mother had founded the convent.

At first Henrietta Maria lived in considerable splendour. Owing to the generosity and kindness of the Queen-Regent Anne of Austria, daughter of Philip III of Spain, she was granted a pension of thirty thousand livres a month, and provided with apartments in the Louvre, also the use of the Palace of St. Germain as a country residence. The boy king Louis XIV had been born there in 1638. Gradually, however, she became impoverished, for she was desperately anxious to help her husband Charles I in England. All the plate and jewels she possessed were sold to supply him with funds. Madame de Motteville, who was a lady-in-waiting to Anne of Austria and on very friendly terms with the exiled Queen, tells us in her *Mémoires*[4] that Henrietta Maria had been obliged to sell almost all her precious stones (*pierreries*). Madame de Motteville felt much compassion for the Queen. Despite her harrowing experiences

Henrietta Maria never became embittered. Surrounded by her ladies, she liked best to talk nostalgically about the happy days she had passed at the English Court, the beauty of the country-side and delighted her audience as of old with her witty sallies. Then with a sudden change of mood tears would pour down her cheeks as she reflected about her straitened means and the danger confronting the King in England.

France had her own troubles during these tumultuous years (1,648–52), the civil war known as the Wars of the Fronde, thus making it almost impossible for the Queen-regent to continue her generous help to her sister-in-law and her daughter. The word Fronde means a Catapult, and the Frondeurs were critics or opponents of the government. It was the most formative in-fluence in the impressionable mind of the boy king Louis XIV, now aged ten. The ignominy of being at times at the mercy of the Paris mob gave him a lasting distaste for that City. Once in early 1649 Louis, together with his mother, had been com-pelled to leave Paris and retire to St. Germain. The leaders in the second war of the Fronde were the great Prince de Condé, the Victor of Rocroi, arrogant, but a brilliant soldier, his brother-in-law the Duc de Longueville, the King's treacherous Uncle Gaston, Duc d'Orléans and his daughter Anne-Marie-Louise, Duchesse de Montpensier, better known later as La Grande Mademoiselle. As a mature young king when first tast-ing the pleasure of absolute power Louis already realized the danger from over-mighty subjects. He was anxious to set up the headquarters of the French monarchy at Versailles, and preferred his courtiers to be dependent on his favour rather than as potentates.

Louis and his mother might leave Paris, but Queen Henrietta Maria and Princess Henrietta remained in their apartments at the Louvre.

The winter of 1648–9 when France was stricken by the first Fronde war or Fronde of the Parliament was particularly severe. Snow was falling in the Paris streets. It was a desolate scene. The groans of wounded men, their cries of despair, penetrated the palace. One day in early January the Queen and Henrietta shivering with cold received an important visitor, the powerful Cardinal de Retz. Madame de Motteville relates in her *Mémoires* that the Cardinal had come to inquire about the well-being of the royal ladies during this time of strife. He found Henrietta Maria by the bedside of the Princess. 'You see me keeping my Henriette company,' said the Queen, 'the poor child has not been able to get up today because there is no fire' (*faute de feu*). The Cardinal de Retz wrote to a correspondent: 'You will do me the justice to believe that Madame d'Angle-terre did not stay next day in bed for want of a fire.'[5] He was not only a humane statesman but a compassionate man. To his eternal honour he pleaded the Queen's case with such success that the Parliament of Paris immediately enacted that 40,000 livres should be sent to Queen Henrietta Maria, for her present use. 'Posterity,' the Cardinal observed with slight irony in his *Mémoires*, 'will hardly believe that a Queen of England and a grand-daughter of Henri Quatre (Princess Henrietta) wanted firewood in the month of January, in the Louvre.' Not without reason Madame de Motteville remarked in her *Mémoires*: 'In that year (1648–9), a terrible star reigned against kings.'

Worse was to follow. Members of the Queen's household learnt during the first part of February (1649) that King Charles I had been executed in Whitehall on 30 January, but they did not dare to tell their mistress. Only later did she learn the terrible truth from her intimate friend, Lord Jermyn (later Earl of St. Albans), a courtier very well disposed towards France. Many feared that the news would drive her insane. Père Cyprien de Gamaches tried to console the Queen. He relates that it was the childish prattle of Princess Henrietta, too young to understand the tragedy, that was her mother's greatest con-solation. For a time the Queen retired to the Carmelite Convent of the Faubourg St. Jacques, then with her customary courage, went to St. Germain. Henceforward she referred to herself as La reine malheureuse in her letters.

During these years of adversity, the young exiled Prince of

Wales later Charles II was often in Paris from 1646 onwards. At sixteen we see him through the eyes of his cousin Anne-Marie-Louise d'Orléans, Mademoiselle as she was called.[5] A great heiress, she had been born at the Louvre on 29 May 1627, and lost her mother, the first wife of Gaston Duc D'Orléans five days after her birth. She was an ambitious intriguer, certainly tactless by temperament, and may have resented that she had not been born a boy. In her *Mémoires*[6] she revealed marked literary ability. La Grande Mademoiselle certainly had a high opinion of herself. In her *Mémoires* she described her fine figure (*belle taille*), her dazzling complexion and fair hair. She is as patronizing about the young Prince of Wales as she was later to be about his sister Princess Henrietta of England. Charles at sixteen was not a particularly prepossessing personality, not at all the popular idea of Charles II as King. He was tall for his age, over six feet in height, with a fine figure, swarthy complexion, dark expressive eyes, and an ugly sensual mouth. He had a slight stammer reminiscent of his father, and his French was so poor in those days that he was obliged to employ his Cousin Prince Rupert of the Rhine as an interpreter. He almost certainly lacked self-confidence. His mother encouraged him to pay court to this lady, for she already designed that he should marry her. Mademoiselle de Montpensier,[7] who had inherited the vast estates of the House of Guise from her mother, had very different ideas. However, she was condescending enough, allowing the callow prince to hand her to her coach and to hold a flambeau before her to lighten her way. She listened rather haughtily to his insincere compliments, but was flattered by his evident desire to please.

It was only after Charles II returned to France after the disastrous Battle of Worcester (1651) that Mademoiselle deigned to look more kindly at her suitor. Charles had found his manhood. Although his rich black hair had been shorn off to complete his disguise after Worcester, he was now more self-assured and had an air of distinction. His French was now fluent. Like his mother, he delighted in witty conversation and he was soon giving his cousin an amusing account of the dangers he had undergone before escaping from England. Mademoiselle de Montpensier noticed how glad he was to return to a civilized country after the rigours he had endured in Scotland. Only when Charles made her proposals of marriage did the haughty lady plainly show that she was not interested in marrying a king who was one only in name. At this period she had aspirations to become Louis XIV's Queen.

To his little sister Henrietta, fourteen years younger than her brother, Charles was from the first a hero of romance. She had been brought up to regard him with some awe as her King, but he showed her even then how deeply attached he was to her. He preferred to conceal his cares from others under a mask of nonchalance, but she sensed his sadness even when a child, and longed to help him. He liked to play with her, and she called him 'Your Majesty' so often he would laugh merrily and say that they must not stand on such ceremony. Henrietta grew to love this tall fascinating brother more deeply than anybody else, even than her mother. In many ways they were affinities, sharing the same interests, both having a marked taste for music and dancing. Henrietta even as a little girl was quick-witted and had a lively imagination. The friendship fostered between brother and sister during the dark years of adversity in France was to be the most constant of their lives. Many men were later to fall madly in love with Henrietta after her marriage to Monsieur the Duc d'Orléans, but she had given her heart to her brother in her childhood and what she later cherished most deeply in her life was his well-being and to bring about an alliance between Britain and France.

After the wars of the Fronde were over, Queen Anne of Austria renewed her pension to her sister-in-law Queen Henrietta and provided for her and her daughter a suite of rooms in the Palais-Royal. This was the palace of Cardinal Richelieu, the Minister of Louis XIII. He had commissioned Le Mercier to build it in 1632. All that remains of the Cardinal's Palace today is the Valois side gallery known as the Prow gallery because of its nautical decoration.

Henrietta Maria preferred to live in the Louvre because it was more peaceful. Perhaps she felt happier at the house she had bought on the heights of Chaillot near Paris overlooking the Seine. She invited ten or twelve nuns from the Convent of the Filles de Marie to live here. Its Abbess was a celebrated lady, Louise de La Fayette, who had once been adored by Louis XIII, though his love for her was platonic.

There Queen Henrietta was fond of retiring with her daughter, sometimes for several weeks. The Princess endeared herself to the Lady Abbess and the nuns by her charm, her natural behaviour and her readiness to wait upon them at table.

It was at Chaillot in her childhood that Henrietta first met Madame de La Fayette,[11] a great literary personality with whom she was to form an intimate friendship. Madame de La Fayette was related to Louise de La Fayette, mère Angelique as she was now called and sometimes visited her there.

When King Louis XIV was sixteen years of age, the French Court became gay and sparkling. He was of fair height, handsome, and his courtesy and graciousness were praised by the courtiers. So courteous was he that he would even take off his hat to a chamber maid. St. Simon, who was sometimes unjust to Louis, later wrote of him with a blend of admiration and malice: 'Never was there a man so naturally polite, nor of such strictly measured politeness, strict by degrees, nor who better distinguished age, merit, rank.' He danced extremely well, and was fond of acting. From boyhood he was majestic, giving the impression that he was born to be a king. Louis had a voracious appetite for food and consequently suffered from indigestion. His love for detail and routine indicated that he had Spanish blood.

Princess Henrietta made her first public appearance at Louis's Court when she was nine years old. It was during February 1654 at a ball given by Cardinal Mazarin to celebrate the marriage of his niece, Anne-Marie Martinozzi to the Prince de Conti. During March the Princess took part in a ballet, and even at that tender age she was much admired. The ballet was entitled 'The Nuptials of Thetis and Peleus' at the Théâtre du Petit Bourbon. The music was by the Italian Lulli, who had been taken into the King's service, having an exquisite talent for the violin, while the verses were by Benserade. Among the actors were Monsieur, younger brother of the King, and his favourite the Comte de Guiche. Olympia Mancini, one of the nieces of the powerful Cardinal Mazarin had a part in the ballet, and the King was reputed to be in love with her. Louis made a magnificent appearance as Apollo, the sun-god, surrounded by the nine muses. Then it was Princess Henrietta's turn to step forward, an enchanting little girl, who spoke the verses written by Benserade so naturally and gracefully:

> *Ma race est du plus pur sang,*
> *Des dieux, et sur nos montagnes,*
> *On me voit tenir un rang*
> *Tout autre que mes compagnes.*
> *Mon jeune et royal aspect*
> *Inspire avec le respect,*
> *La pitoyable tendresse,*
> *Et c'est à moi qu'on s'adresse,*
> *Quand on veut plaindre tout haut*
> *Le sort des grandes personnes*
> *Et dire tout ce qu'il faut*
> *Sur la chute des couronnes.*

At this period Queen Anne of Austria was much attached to the Princess Henrietta, and even indulged in the hope that her son the King might marry the Princess of England. The project most dear to Anne of Austria was that the King of France should marry one of the Spanish Infantas, her nieces. The political situation at present made this impossible because France and Spain were still engaged in a long war. Louis, however, was not at all attracted to his cousin Princess Henrietta, who he regarded as a mere child. The sensual young King had no eyes for anybody except the voluptuous nieces of Cardinal Mazarin. When she gazed at her elder son the King, the devout Anne of Austria must have thought of her own special church of Val-de-Grâce in the Porte Royale district of Paris. After twenty-three years of childlessness, Louis XIII's Queen at last had given birth to the heir to the throne. In gratitude she had vowed that she would build a magnificent church, and plans for the edifice were drawn by François Mansart. There it stands today, beautiful and timeless, with its strong Baroque influence and exquisite cupola by Pierre Mignard, a memorial to a queen and a mother, who had once longed for a son. Later when she was Madame, the wife of Queen Anne's younger son, the Princess d'Angleterre would sometimes accompany her mother-in-law to Val-de-Grâce.

Nothing is more humiliating to an exile than to have to accept the charity of others. Although Anne of Austria was invariably kind and generous, Henriette and her mother were occasionally subjected to slights and rebuffs at the French Court. Such an occasion occurred at a small informal dance at the Louvre during the winter of 1655 when Henriette and her mother were guests of the Queen-Mother. Madame de Motteville refers to the incident in her *Mémoires*. As soon as the violins struck up, Louis hastened to ask the Cardinal's niece, the Duchesse de Mercoeur, to dance with him. Embarrassment showed on many faces. Anne of Austria amazed at this lapse from etiquette, whispered that he must dance the first dance with the Princess of England. The young King replied sulkily 'I do not like little girls.' Henrietta Maria tactfully tried to smooth matters by saying that her daughter had hurt her foot and could not dance. Anne of Austria then said if the Princess could not dance, neither should the King.

Small wonder if Henriette did not feel offended and now declared that she did not want to dance. Finally the King and the Princess of England, now eleven, were forced by the joint persuasions of their mothers into a sulky acquiescence as Madame de Motteville relates. This is really an isolated in-

24

stance, and the King usually treated Henrietta Maria and her daughter with courtesy, though other members of the Royal Family were not so considerate.

Early during 1654 England and France signed a Treaty of Alliance. Cromwell insisted that one of its conditions should be observed, that Charles II must leave France. He now sought refuge at Cologne. His mother Queen Henrietta Maria now revealed a less attractive aspect of her character. For some time the Queen had been doing her utmost to convert her younger son Henry of Oatlands Duke of Gloucester to the Roman Catholic religion. For this purpose she was supported by her recently appointed Almoner Abbe Walter Montagu, a son of the First Earl of Manchester. He was Abbot of St. Martin de Pontoise. Montagu had all the fiery zeal of a recent convert for he had been won over by the Jesuits to the Roman Catholic religion during a visit to Paris. Despite Queen Henrietta's solemn promise to Charles II that she would not attempt to convert the boy duke, she sent him to Pontoise where she hoped he would be persuaded by her almoner to enter the Jesuit's College. When he heard what his mother intended, Charles was very indignant and wrote on 10 November 1654 from Cologne urging his brother to hold fast to the Protestant religion.

> Dear Brother, [he wrote][8] I have received yours without a date in which you mention that Mr. Montagu [the Abbe] has endeavoured to pervert you in yr religion ... yet the letters that come from Paris say, that it is the Queen's purpose to do all she can to change yr religion, which if you hearken to her, or anybody else in that matter you must never thinke to see England or me againe. ...

He reminded the Duke of Gloucester of the last words of his dear father, to be constant to his religion. The Princess of Orange from Holland and even the Duke of York gave their moral support to their brother in his determination to remain a Protestant.

One day when his mother was just about to start for Chaillot in her coach, the boy Duke—he was called 'Little Mr. Harry' by the Royalists—knelt before her to crave her farewell blessing. The Queen, however, harshly told him to begone and that she never wished to see his face again. Prince Henry was extremely upset. Meanwhile Princess Henrietta much bewildered by the turn of events and torn between love of her mother and her deep attachment to her young brother tenderly embraced him in the Palais-Royal. The child cried bitterly: 'Oh me, my brother! Oh me, my mother! What shall I do? I am undone for ever.' Gloucester joined the King in Cologne. His early death was a great loss to the Stuart cause.

Princess Henrietta's tastes were literary and artistic. She took a special delight in music and poetry. Not only did she sing well, but she played the guitar and harpsichord with considerable feeling and she was an exquisite and graceful dancer. These accomplishments especially delighted her brother King Charles. So, those early years gradually passed. She was her mother's constant companion at the Palais-Royal, and there were frequent visits to Chaillot, and more occasional ones to Colombes, a pretty country house on the Seine where they would usually go in the summer. It was from Colombes that the Princess wrote a few of her earliest letters to her brother Charles. For the sake of her health Henrietta Maria occasionally went to Bourbon to drink the waters.

For a lively, pleasure-loving princess, life was sometimes tedious, but the monotony was relieved by the visit of her elder sister Mary, Princess of Orange to France. This occurred during the winter of 1656. The ostensible purpose was to heal the breach caused by her mother's attempts to convert the Duke of Gloucester and to effect a reconciliation between her brother Charles II and his mother. The Princess Royal, who possessed much of the animation and gaiety of Charles, was generous to him, giving him money and visiting him whenever possible at Cologne. Mary was very well received at the French Court, and hospitably entertained. Even La Grande Mademoiselle was impressed by Princess Mary, especially by the beauty of the pearls and diamonds which she wore. She talked incessantly to La Grande Mademoiselle telling her how much she liked the Court of France. She had, however, a terrible aversion for Holland. So soon as her brother was re-established on his throne she would go to live with him. Meanwhile she enjoyed herself enormously. When Louis XIV's Chancellor gave a great fête for her during the carnival time she only regretted that she could not dance because etiquette forbade her as a widow* to dance at Anne of Austria's Court. Instead, after the Chancellor had led his guests through a gallery illuminated with 300 torches, the King opened the ball with Princess Henrietta, looking so pretty that she seemed an angel on earth. Her dancing was so perfect that she was greatly admired. As for the Princess of Orange, though her mother could not resist trying to convert her and insisted on taking her to the Carmelite Convent she turned a deaf ear when her mother broached the subject.

It is curious how much the ladies of high birth were influenced by Questions of precedence and etiquette in the seventeenth century. La Grande Mademoiselle mentions in her *Mémoires* a magnificent fête given by the Chancellor Seguier during the Carnival of 1658. In her maddening, patronizing way Mademoiselle de Montpensier wrote: 'The Queen (Henrietta Maria) brought La Princesse d'Angleterre poor child, she was enchanted to be there, since she only goes to balls at the Louvre as a rule.' The Queen-Mother complained that Mademoiselle had passed before the Princesse d'Angleterre to supper. When Cardinal Mazarin scolded Mademoiselle de Montpensier for her presumption she was defended by her cousin Monsieur (Philippe d'Orléans), who said—'And if she did, she was perfectly right! Things must have come to a pretty pass, if we are to allow people who depend upon us for bread to pass before us.' A remark in very bad taste for which he was rebuked by his mother Anne of Austria. The Cardinal was more tactful, for knowing how proud Mademoiselle was he hastened to assure

*She was the mother of the future William III.

27

her that in older times the Kings of Scotland had always yielded precedence to the sons of France.

Tallemant des Reaux in his *Historiettes*[9]—an entertaining book, but by no means always truthful—refers to the Chancelier Pierre Seguier in a very disdainful way as a man who was too avid of praise (louanges). His habits were dirty. 'He eats in a most slovenly manner,' he wrote. Whatever were Seguier's failings as a politician—and he occupied a high position for many years—he was, a man of learning. France owes to him L'Academie Française at least as much as she owes it to Cardinal Richelieu. He had a very fine library, which he later bequeathed to the Abbey of St. Germain-des-Près.

It was Giulio Mazarin, the Italian-born eldest son of Pietro Mazarini of Palermo and of Ortensia Bufalini, who enjoyed the real power in France during these years. His relations with Queen Anne of Austria were very intimate—some alleged they were lovers. His chief vice was his insatiable love of money but he had a refined taste for all the exquisite works of art he had collected even if he had been unscrupulous sometimes in obtaining them. His policy during the years 1657–8 was to form a close alliance with Oliver Cromwell, who sent a detachment of his Ironsides to support Marechal de Turenne in his campaign against Spanish Flanders.

During 1657 Olympia Mancini who had so attracted the young King Louis and shared his taste for amateur theatricals, married Eugène Maurice Prince of Savoie-Carignan. A brave soldier with a passion for hunting, he later became the Comte de Soissons.[10] Louis now became infatuated with Olympia's younger more intellectual sister Marie, who was passionately in love with him and even aspired to be his Queen. Anne of Austria regarded her son's infatuation for the Cardinal's niece with dismay and told Cardinal Mazarin she would never consent to such a mésalliance. Her choice for her son's queen was the Princess of England, but it may be that his mother's subtle hints that she would make him a suitable bride set him against the idea. Then with the signing of the Treaty of the Pyrenees

(7 November 1659), which ended the long war between France and Spain, the project of Louis's marriage to the Infanta Marie-Thérèse, daughter of Philip IV of Spain, was revived. With the death of Oliver Cromwell during September 1658 Charles II might well hope that he would be speedily restored to his throne, but his hopes were doomed to disappointment. In an attempt to acquire the sympathy of Cardinal Mazarin, Charles now asked for the hand of Hortense Mancini, the youngest and most beautiful of his nieces and reputed to be his favourite. The Abbé Montagu in particular supported this project and Queen Henrietta, too, was eager that it should be embraced, but the Cardinal gave evasive replies couched in diplomatic language, saying that the King of England did him too much honour. With slight irony he inferred that while the King's cousin Mademoiselle de Montpensier remained unmarried he really must not think of marrying a mere demoiselle.

III

Brother and Sister

Madame de Motteville relates in her *Mémoires* that Princess Henriette was disappointed that she did not become Queen of France, and that may well be true. Up to the age of fifteen there was still a chance that she might one day be the bride of Louis XIV. A French lady Madame de Brégis describes her at this period in a rather artificial style.

> To begin with her height, I must tell you that this young Princess is still growing and that she will soon attain a perfect stature. Her air is as noble as her birth, her hair is of a bright chestnut hue, and her complexion rivals that of the gayest flowers. The snowy whiteness of her skin betrays the lilies from which she sprang. Her eyes are blue and brilliant, her lips ruddy, her throat beautiful, her arms and hands well made. Her charms show that she was born on a throne, and is destined to return there. Her wit is lively and agreeable. She is admired in her serious moments and beloved in her most ordinary ones; she is gentle and obliging, and her kindness of heart will not allow her to laugh at others, as cleverly as she could if she chose. She spends most of her time in learning, all that can make a princess perfect, and devotes her spare moments to the most varied accomplishments. She dances with incomparable grace, she sings like an angel, and the spinet is never so well played as by her fair hands....

The Abbé de Choisy, another contemporary, differs from Madame de Brégis in describing the Princess of England's eyes as dark. It is curious that nobody mentions in her childhood

30

that she was fond of riding, for she was to become an accomplished horsewoman.

One defect she had in her figure was so artfully concealed that nobody suspected it. One of her shoulders was slightly higher than the other. Mademoiselle de Montpensier, who was jealous of the Princess in the early days, could not resist writing in her *Mémoires* that even her husband was unaware of it until after his marriage.

The Yorkshire Squire Sir John Reresby, who was in Paris during the winter (1658–9) recovering from a serious illness managed to visit Queen Henrietta Maria and her daughter in the Palais Royal without much notice being taken of it in England. He was favourably impressed by the Princess. He wrote in his memoirs:

> Besides speaking the language of that country and dancing passably well the young Princess then aged about fifteen, used me with all the civil freedom that might be, made me dance with her, played on the harpsichord to me in her Highness's chamber, suffered me to attend upon her as she walked in the garden with the rest of the retinue.[1]

She even allowed him to toss her in a swing made of a cable— a delightful touch this—and Sir John relates that he was present at most of her innocent diversions.

Her greatest joy were the rare visits of her brother Charles. Strange as it may seem the weary exile had not seen his sister for several years when he arrived in Colombes on 5 December 1659 to stay with her and his mother. He first embraced his mother, looked around for the little sister he so much cherished and was about to kiss another young girl when one of his courtiers My Lord Gerard pointed out his mistake. With shy reverence there came towards him an exquisite faun-like delicate young lady of fifteen, very thin it is true, but so much changed from the little girl he had played with at Chaillot or in the Palais-Royal that Charles could not conceal his surprise and delight. Hester Chapman in her book *The Tragedy of Charles*

31

II wrote that the King 'liked to bask in his dear, dearest Minette's uncritical adoration'.[2] This may be true when she was very young, but Henrietta was as strong a personality as her beloved brother and she was later never afraid to give him her mind, though it was done with exquisite tact, even if her views differed from his. Hester Chapman underrated the princess's intelligence and her cleverness. To dismiss her as silly-clever is too facile. A close study of Henrietta's original letters in the Lambeth Palace Library and the Public Record Office shows that she had an extremely good political brain and many of the qualities of a skilled diplomat. She was not intellectual, but she possessed an instinctive literary critical faculty.

The twelve days Charles passed in the society of his sister were of enormous significance to both of them. Not only in fostering the tender devotion between Charles and Henrietta, but also of importance to the destinies of England and France. Now for the first time Charles called his sister by his pet nickname of Minette. It was a name very sparingly used and by him alone so far as we know. In France before her marriage to Monsieur she is referred to as La Princesse d'Angleterre and after her marriage always as Madame. In Charles's original letters to his sister, mostly in the archives of the Quai D'Orsay he calls her ma chère Minette several times and in one of her letters to him she alludes to herself as '*votre pauvre Minette*'. Queen Henrietta Maria when writing to her son Charles II usually refers to Henriette as her daughter. Unfortunately all her correspondence with the Princess has been either lost or destroyed.

Princess Henrietta's first known letter to her brother Charles is in the Archbishop of Canterbury's library in Lambeth Palace. It is very charming. All her twenty-three letters in the Archbishop's library are written in French, for she could scarcely write English. Only one of her letters is in that language. Its spelling is very quaint. It is written to Sir Thomas Clifford,[3] one of her brother's chief ministers, a member of the celebrated Cabal.

Brother and Sister

She was aged fifteen when she wrote her first letter during 1659 to Charles. Her brother had travelled to Fuenterrabia in Spain where he hoped to unite both France and Spain in his efforts to be restored to the throne.

I would not let my Lord Inchiquin leave without assuring Your Majesty of the respect I have for you [wrote his sister]. You do me too much favour in writing so often. I fear it must give you trouble and I should be grieved that Your Majesty should take so much trouble for a little sister who is not worthy of it, but who can realise this honour and rejoice in it. I hope that the Peace (The Treaty of the Pyrenees signed 7 November 1659] will give you all the happiness [bonheur] you can desire and I should rejoice in it because of the love and respect I have for Your Majesty. This is a great joy to me since it gives me the hope of seeing Your Majesty, which is a thing passionately desired by your very humble servant.[4]

Henrietta's letters are invariably unsigned: Murrough O'Brien 1st Earl of Inchiquin was the confidential bearer of this letter to Charles in Spain.

It is evident that Charles had been writing often to his sister, but these early letters must be lost. While Henrietta was an excellent correspondent, Charles was on the whole an indolent writer of letters. However, he found time soon after his departure from Colombes to write to his sister on 20 December. This correspondence casts a very favourable light on the character of Charles II.

The kindnesse I have for you will not permit me [he wrote] to loose this occasion to conjure you to continue your kindnesse to a brother that loves you more than he can expresse, which truth I hope you are so well persuaded of, as I, may expect these returns which I shall strive to deserve, deare sister be kinde to me, and be confident that I am intierly yours.

Charles's signature is always difficult to read, but it is presumably C. The letter is endorsed For my Deare Sister the Princess Henriette.[5]

Charles's second known letter to his sister illustrates the charm of the man, and shows that the tastes of brother and sister were very similar. He wrote from Brussels on 7 February 1660, three months before the Restoration.

> I begin this letter in French by assuring you that I do not mind your scolding me (*vous me grondes*). I give in joyfully since you quarrel so charmingly with me, but I will never give up the friendship that I have for you, and you give me so many marks of yours that we shall never have any other quarrel but as which of us shall love the other most, but in this I will never yield to you. I send you this by the hands of Janton who is the best girl in the world. We talk of you every day and wish a thousand times in the day to be with you. Her voice has almost entirely come back and she sings very well. She has taught me La Chanson de ma Queu, 'I preetily sweete harte come tell me and do not lie', and a number of others. When you send me the scapulary I promise to wear it always for love of you. Tell Mme. Borde that I will send her my portrait soon ... Let me know, I pray, how you pass your time, for if you have been at Chaillot in this inclement weather you will have found it somewhat tedious. In future I beg of you do not treat me with so much ceremony in according me so many 'Majesties', for I do not wish there to be anything else between us two but friendship.

The letter is endorsed For deare deare Sister.[6] Charles's messenger bearing his letter to his sister was almost certainly French, the charming Janton who sang so well. Mme. des Bordes was the Princess's devoted attendant and femme de chambre throughout her short life and was with her at the end. It is absolutely natural that these early letters should touch on their mutual love of music rather than the momentous political matters that occupied his mind.

Brother and Sister

Charles now entered into secret negotiations with General George Monk (he had this in common with the King's sister that he was also a Devon man) for his return to his Kingdom. With his innate caution Monk did not pursue a decisive policy until the Rump Parliament had voted its own dissolution. He now wrote to Charles advising him to join his sister Princess Mary of Orange at Breda, where he issued a Declaration, promising a general amnesty and religious toleration if he were restored to his Kingdom. Charles had learnt much in the harsh school of adversity, and he had acquired his knowledge not from books, but from intercourse with all types of men. No wonder he had acquired a cynical realism, to be an enormous asset to him as King of England. He never forgave the States of Holland for their churlish treatment during his exile, and ever afterwards had an unshakeable dislike for Dutchmen. He had no illusions when the States of Holland loaded him with presents. It was now a foregone conclusion that the new Parliament would restore him to his Kingdom.

Meanwhile he did not once mention these weighty matters to his little sister Henriette in his letter from Breda, but wrote to tell her how deeply he loved her. His tastes were French. He wanted the fashionable Parisian tailor, Claude Sourceau to make him a suit, and thought so highly of him that Sourceau later became royal tailor in London. 'I have given him orders to bring you some ribbon, so that you may choose the trimmings and the feathers,' he told Minette, 'I thank you for the song you have sent me. I do not know if it is pretty, for Janton does not know it yet.'[7] There was a fundamental loneliness about Charles despite the hordes of place-seekers who now besieged him. He liked somebody near him to talk about his sister.

Commissioners now arrived at Breda for the purpose of inviting the King to return, bringing with them £30,000 in gold, much to the delight of Charles II, Mary of Orange and the Duke of York. Then the King embarked on the *Naseby* for the journey to Dover, and the ship was now named the Royal Charles. At Dover he was received by General Monk and the nobility and gentry. To the Mayor of Dover after he had presented His Majesty with a fine bible he said that he loved it above all things in the world. Then with the acclamations of the people ringing in his ears, Charles entered his coach to drive to Canterbury.

There, despite the welter and press of business while the bells of Canterbury Cathedral sounded sweet in the air, Charles found time to write a short letter to his sister, entrusting it to Edward Progers, a favourite retainer, to carry it to France. He told her that he was sending her a little present, having instructed his sister the Princess of Orange to make the necessary arrangements. Actually it was a most elegant side-saddle with trappings of green velvet embroidered with gold lace. 'My head is so prodigiously dazed by the acclamation of the people and by quantities of business', wrote her brother, 'that I know not whether I am writing sense or not ...' and Henriette's excitement and joy when Mr. Progers arrived at Colombes with her brother's letter. She idolized him. What pleasure it gave her that he had remembered her.

IV

Monsieur

There was no lack of eligible suitors for the hand of the Princess
Henriette in marriage once her brother had been restored to
the throne, although neither the Duke of Savoy nor the heir to
the Grand Duchy of Tuscany had shown the slightest desire
to pursue the matter further while Henriette was a penniless
princess. For some time, however, before Charles II's Restoration, Monsieur Philippe Duc d'Orléans had been ardently in
love with the Princess, and he had persuaded the Princess
Palatine, Anne de Gonzague, wife of Prince Edward, youngest
son of Elizabeth Queen of Bohemia to press his suit. Cardinal
Mazarin had been strongly averse to the marriage of the heir
presumptive to the throne of France with the impoverished
sister of an exiled king. Once Charles had regained his throne
he supported the project. King Louis now married to the Infanta Marie-Thérèse was well aware of his brother's infatuation
for the Princess of England, and not without a touch of cruelty
was in the habit of indulging in raillery and mockery when discussing the matter with Philippe. 'You will marry the Princess
of England,' he would tell him, 'for nobody else wants her.
Monsieur de Savoie has refused her and I have had Monsieur
de Florence sounded about her; they neither of them want her.'
According to Mademoiselle de Montpensier (La Grande
Mademoiselle), Louis told his brother that he ought not to
hurry to marry the bones of the Holy Innocents— a distasteful
reference to Henriette's thinness. Not without a trace of feminine spite she would mention in her *Mémoires* that Madame was
slightly hump-backed (*bossue*). Mademoiselle de Montpensier
had no desire to marry Philippe herself, but she was possessive

by nature and was certainly piqued that her cousin should so eagerly desire to marry the Princess of England. As for Philippe, Mademoiselle was repelled by his effeminacy, but the contrast in their characters and the marked masculine vein in her own nature responded to Philippe's superficial cleverness, and his nimble wit. Although too aware of Monsieur's many defects, she retained a certain liking for him. Nothing gave Monsieur such exquisite pleasure as to disguise himself as a nun at a masquerade. When a monk had tried to make love to him, he was highly delighted that the man had lovely white feminine hands. Mademoiselle pretended to disguise herself as a warrior in silver armour.

Philippe was two years younger than Louis, having been born on 21 September 1640. He received the title of Duc d'Anjou. That strange man his father Louis XIII had shown signs of pleasure at the birth of his younger son, though his countenance had remained grave when his Queen Anne of Austria had given birth to the heir to the throne. A Te-Deum was chanted at Notre-Dame to celebrate Philippe's birth. Pierre Mignard's fine portrait at Versailles shows that Monsieur was not unhandsome in early manhood, though his mouth was too small and his nose too large.

He was so small and slight that he felt obliged to wear shoes with heels so high that he seemed to be on stilts. His hair was pitch-black and curly and his teeth were very white. His eyes were large and brown. He spent a lot of time attending to his toilet concentrating on powdering his hair, rouging his cheeks and loading himself with ribbons and jewels. Monsieur had a taste for interior decorating and his inclinations were more artistic than his brother. He was a discriminating and indefatigable collector of Dutch pictures, an interest certainly not shared by the King.[1] Monsieur was an enthusiastic collector of rare and precious things, porcelain from China, lacquer, silver plate and above all, precious stones (*pierreries*). Like Mademoiselle de Montpensier he was quite an authority on precedence. The fussy little man would discuss it incessantly, and he took a great interest in Ceremonial. La Grande Mademoiselle relates that when her father Gaston Duc d'Orléans died during February 1660, King Louis remarked to her:

> Tomorrow you will see Monsieur in a trailing violet mantle. He is enchanted to hear of your father's death, so as to have the pleasure of wearing one. It is lucky for me that I am older than he is, or he would have been longing for my death!

The brothers, however, were very fond of one another, although Philippe would complain that Monsieur (so he called the King) did not treat him seriously, with a kind of affectionate contempt, like a pet poodle. Despite his defects, his malicious tongue and his vanity, mentioned by Saint-Simon, his pleasure in spreading scandal and making mischief, Monsieur did not lack personal courage.

It is easy to dismiss Monsieur as odious and even vicious, but one can almost feel pity for the man. Compassion, no, it is too strong a word. His mother Queen Anne of Austria and Cardinal Mazarin were responsible for his upbringing and they must share the blame for shaping his character in the early years, and encouraging his effeminacy. Their main purpose was to prevent the younger prince from becoming a dangerous rival to King Louis as Gaston had undoubtedly been to his brother Louis XIII. Therefore manly pursuits were discouraged and any inclinations he might have to assert himself too vigorously were stifled in boyhood. The courtiers might find Philippe's waspish intelligence irritating, but on the whole they rather liked him. There was even a rumour that Philippe, whose features were somewhat Italian, was really the son of Cardinal Mazarin.

If many were aware at Court that Monsieur was addicted to boyish vices and was in fact a homosexual, others undoubtedly hoped that marriage to the slender, graceful, enchanting Princess would rid him of these inclinations. Besides it would create a personal link with France. Henriette herself had no aversion to marriage with Philippe, though she was not in the least in love with him. The Marriage with Monsieur would mean that she would remain in France, and from infancy she had been brought up in that country with French as her natural language. The Queen-Mother, Anne of Austria was extremely pleased, thinking mistakenly as it transpired that she would acquire a docile daughter-in-law. Queen Henrietta Maria was delighted, reflecting no doubt that her beloved daughter would still remain near her. Furthermore, since she could not have the King as son-in-law (he had married the Infanta of Spain at St. Jean-de-Luz) she considered Monsieur an excellent match. Since the death of Gaston, Louis had invested his brother with the Duchies of Orléans, Valois and Chartres. He had been given country estates at St. Cloud, Villers-Cotterets near Laon and Montergis.

Many cavaliers well aware that Princess Henriette possessed considerable influence with the King of England begged her to write to him on their behalf. Typical of these was one she wrote from Colombes on 30 June 1660, supporting some petition Charles Boyle, Viscount Dungarvan, eldest son of the Earl of Cork, who was the bearer of the letter of Charles II, wanted to present to the King. The Princess wrote her brother that the Queen her mother would have herself written, but that she had eaten some fruit, which had upset her stomach. 'God be praised it is not a dangerous malady,' she told him. Henrietta Maria was particularly interested in this nobleman because he was the nephew of her principal Lady of the Bedchamber (the widow of Lewis Boyle, Viscount Kinalmeaky, who had been killed at the Battle of Liscarrol in 1642). This letter is in the Lambeth Palace Collection.[2] The remains of the blue seal with her coat of arms as a Princess of Great Britain and Ireland prove that it was written before her marriage.

Throughout the summer (1660) Monsieur grew more and more impatient that the marriage negotiations should proceed more speedily. Henrietta Maria thought it politic while asking for Charles II's informal consent to the marriage to stress that

Monsieur

Monsieur was very much in love.[3] There were a great number of festivities during that summer. Monsieur was host at a magnificent ball at his new country home at St. Cloud and he opened the ball with the Princess Henriette, who was wearing a new white dress, sewn all over with pearls and diamonds. She danced divinely. Cardinal Mazarin gave, too, a sumptuous banquet in their honour. Looking a little nervous and hardly able to take his eyes off his betrothed, Philippe led in the Princess garbed in the same white dress like a bride.

In her correspondence with her brother, Henriette reveals an agreeable sense of humour. Among the Lambeth Palace letters is one written on 17 August 1661 introducing a Frenchman Monsieur Février or Féburier who was probably a merchant. 'He comes to you with the assurance he has been given that he will be able to cheat more than half the kingdom',[4] she wrote him. According to the Treasury Books and Papers, he was successful in achieving this, for he received as much as £1000 from Thomas Chiffinch for some goods he brought him from France to England, presumably for His Majesty. What is really of most interest is the Princess's reference to the forthcoming state entry into Paris 'of the young Queen' Marie-Thérèse. She told Charles that Harry Jermyn, now Earl of St. Albans, would give an account to the King of this ceremonial event 'and would perform this task rather better than I'.

About a week later Henriette, her mother, the Queen-Mother of France, Cardinal Mazarin and other notabilities witnessed this superb spectacle from the Hôtel de Beauvais in the Rue François-Miron.[5] It is situated in the Marais district of Paris just off the Rue St. Antoine. It was a scorching hot day at the end of August. An Arc de Triomphe had been erected at the gates of St. Antoine. There was the sound of trumpets, the beating of drums, the exultant roaring of the fickle people of Paris. Queen Marie-Thérèse was in her golden chariot, her face placid and rather stupid. On her right side rode King Louis on a white horse, his golden armour glittering in the sunlight, seeming to the crowd to be the Sun-God himself. Henriette's betrothed, Monsieur was a resplendent figure on his white horse, and wearing a richly embroidered suit blazing with jewels. As he passed by he looked up intently at the balcony of the Hôtel de Beauvais as if to seek admiration, even applause from the Princess of England. What were Henriette's thoughts at this moment? Was she carried away by the emotional mood of those around her? Did she really think that after the bitter years of penury and exile that a radiant dawn was about to break? It may well be that a slight feeling of apprehension possessed her for a moment or two as she looked down on Monsieur and his prancing horse, to be chased away, like the ripples in a stream, stirred by a light wind.

The Princess continued to write to King Charles on behalf of Cavaliers such as Colonel John Fitzpatrick, a kinsman of the Earl of Inchiquin and a gallant soldier, who had fought against the rebels in Ireland in 1652. In her sensitive way she was always afraid that her brother might think her importunate in bothering him about these matters when he had a thousand problems to face. Fitzpatrick wanted the restoration of lands of which he had been dispossessed. In the same letter is a jocular reference to Madame de Fiennes, dame d'atours to Queen Henrietta Maria. She was in the habit of taking considerable liberties with Charles II and other members of the royal family. She now asked the Princess to give her brother the message 'that it is fortunate for you she has no army, for if she had she would be revenged on you for talking about her letters without having opened them'.

Despite the transformation in their fortunes, further sorrow was in store for the Stuarts. In the late summer the young Duke of Gloucester, who had accompanied his brothers to England on Charles's restoration, was smitten with smallpox from which he died. The blow was a heavy one for Charles, for Henry was a Prince of high promise. Henriette was also tenderly attached to this brother. She refers to their loss in a letter written on 10 October from Colombes, describing it 'as so cruel a misfortune', although she does not mention Gloucester by name.

She told him in the same letter that the thing she desired most on earth was to have the happiness of seeing him.

At sixteen the Princess Henriette was almost at her best, a radiant, lovely girl. Her great gift was the art of pleasing everybody. Madame de Motteville describes her:

> The Princess of England was above middle height; she was very graceful and her figure, which was not faultless, did not appear so imperfect as it really was. Her beauty was not of the most perfect kind, but her charming manners made her very attractive. She had an extremely delicate and very white skin, with a bright natural colour, a complexion so to speak of roses and jasmine. Her eyes were small, but very soft and sparkling, her nose not bad, her lips were rosy and her teeth as white and regular as you could wish, but her face was too long, and her great thinness seemed to threaten her with early decay [*menacer sa beauté d'une prompte fin*]. She dressed her hair and whole person in a most becoming manner, and she was so lovable in herself that she could not fail to please. She had not been able to become Queen, but to make up for this disappointment she wished to reign in the hearts of all good people by the charm of her person and the real beauty of her soul.

It was arranged during the autumn (1660) that Queen Henrietta Maria and the Princess should visit the King in England, so as to congratulate him on his restoration to the throne. They looked forward to a happy family reunion, for Princess Mary of Orange was also going to London. There were other objects for the journey. It was necessary to decide on a dowry for the Princess. The Queen was also furious that her son the Duke of York contracted a secret marriage with Anne Hyde, the daughter of her old adversary Edward Hyde now Earl of Clarendon, and wanted to get it annulled. Monsieur was in despair at the impending separation from his betrothed.

Among those who accompanied the royal travellers to England, were the Abbé Walter Montagu, the Queen's Grand

Almoner and Père Cyprien de Gamaches, who gave an amusing account of his experiences in his *Mémoires*. There was a dead calm in the channel, and it took two days to reach Dover from Calais where they arrived on 6 November. With a favourable wind this voyage could take two hours. At Dover Charles II was impatiently awaiting his mother and sister. After warmly embracing them, the King conducted them to Dover Castle where together with the Duke and Duchess of York, Princess Mary of Orange, and Prince Rupert of the Rhine they sat down to a splendid banquet.

Père Cyprien was very impressed during the journey by the thoughtfulness of James Duke of York in providing him and the Queen's French servants with fish, although it happened to be a fast day.

Perhaps it was a little tactless of him to rise to his feet at the King's table to recite a Latin grace and to make a great sign of the Cross, though he was possibly ignorant of the strong anti-Catholic prejudice of the mass of the people. It was amusing to see the expressions of surprise and horror on the faces of the townsmen of Dover, for many of them were Puritans and Trembleurs[6] (Quakers). Father Cyprien mentions in his *Mémoires* the blind and criminal aversion that they had for the Roman Catholic Church. The following day high mass was celebrated in the Castle hall. Later the royal party went in coaches by way of Canterbury to Rochester where they spent the night. What most pleased Charles II was the eagerness of the Kentish gentlewomen, who came to see him and persisted in holding up their faces, country-wise, for him to kiss.[7] When the travellers reached Lambeth, they crossed over to Whitehall by boat. Although bells were rung in the churches, comparatively few bonfires were lit. It may well be that the people were not aware of the Queen's arrival in Whitehall, for the original project to make a state entry into the Capital by state barges from Gravesend had been abondoned.

Although the popularity of Henrietta Maria was very doubtful in London, the Princess by her gracious manner and her courtesy won all hearts. John Evelyn, for instance, was enchanted by Princess Henrietta's graciousness in St. James's Palace in thanking his wife 'for the "Character" (*A Character of England*) she had presented her, which was afterwards printed'.[8] To Samuel Pepys, however, the Princess Henrietta seemed very pretty, 'but much below my expectation; and her dressing of herself with her haire frized short up to her eares did make her seem so much the less to me'.[9] His wife was really much handsomer than her. Pepys was impressed when he saw the French ambassador Le Comte de Soissons on his way from Westminster to Whitehall to an audience, 'his own coach all red velvet covered with gold lace, and drawn by six barbes'. This was Prince Eugène Maurice of Savoy, husband of Olympia Mancini.

M. Bartet, the French Ambassador's secretary, accompanied him on 16 November when the King conducted the Comte de Soissons into his sister's private apartments in Whitehall. There he saw her in her cornette (mob-cap) and an Indian cotton robe of a thousand colours playing at Ombre with the Princess of Orange and the Duke of York. 'You can tell Monsieur', he wrote Cardinal Mazarin, 'that he never saw her more beautiful in full dress, than she appeared to me at that moment.'[10]

Poor Monsieur in Paris had grown quite thin and melancholy, and suffered from insomnia in the absence of the Princess. He became even more agitated when reports reached him that George Villiers, Second Duke of Buckingham had fallen madly in love with his betrothed.

Princess Henrietta was immensely popular in England, and members of the nobility vied with one another to entertain her at balls and supper parties. She was happy to be reunited with her beloved brother, but the fugitive days passed much too quickly.

She was ready with a pretty phrase when a deputation from the House of Commons, headed by Mr. Arthur Annesley waited upon her, bearing an address of welcome and a present of £10,000. With exquisite tact and graciousness she received them. The members of the deputation later reported: 'The Princess with great affection acknowledged the kindness of the House, excusing herself that she could not do it so well in the English tongue, which she desired to supply, with an English heart.'[11] Unfortunately Henrietta never received this money. Many years later she informed Ralph Montagu the British Ambassador in France that 'the King made bold with it, and she never had a farthing of it'.

Meanwhile Monsieur was in despair when he heard rumours in France that the Emperor Leopold intended to send a special envoy to ask for the Princess's hand in marriage. There was not the slightest risk that his hopes would be realized. There is a letter among the archives in the Quai D'Orsay showing that the Comte de Soissons was received in audience by Charles II on 20 November and made his formal demand for the hand of the Princess on behalf of King Louis of France for his brother.[12] King Charles officially informed King Louis: 'We find a fresh argument to persuade us thereof in the Embassy made to us by so eminent and honourable a person as the Count of Soissons.' Parliament now voted that the Princess should receive a dowry of £40,000. When Charles had charged the Earl of St. Albans to undertake a special mission to France during July 1660, the French authorities were asked 'to give him every assistance and to be plainly persuaded of the sincerity of all that he will tell you on my part'. Towards the end of the year St. Albans was appointed ambassador extraordinary to France and he was specially instructed to look after the interests of the Princess after she became Duchess of Orléans, Charles II used to say of this intimate adviser of his mother that he was more a Frenchman than an Englishman. His tastes were magnificent and he liked exquisite food. The name of Henry Jermyn Earl of St. Albans today survives in Jermyn Street. During 1664 he obtained a grant of land in Pall Mall and began the planning of St. James's Square.

The Abbé Montagu's favourite project was that King Charles should marry Hortense Mancini, and his mother, too,

Monsieur

supported this match, for Hortense was a Roman Catholic. Besides, she told her son that Cardinal Mazarin was bound to grant his niece an enormous dowry, allowing him to be independent of Parliament. Whether or not the wily cardinal favoured the proposed marriage is at least equivocal, but he certainly did not want to give the impression of doing so. It was opposed by the Chancellor, Lord Clarendon and other of the King's advisers. Nothing came of it.

During those fleeting winter days when Minette was enjoying the companionship of her brother he took the opportunity while they were walking together at Hampton Court, even more beautiful than today basking as it did in the pale sunlight with its warm red brick courtyards, to stress to her the importance of her marriage. Its overriding purpose was to unite England and France so that her brother might be strong against the world. If Minette showed little enthusiasm for her marriage to Monsieur, Charles would reassure her with a touch of his characteristic realism and cynicism when discussing unhappy marriages, that those made for love were the worst since that was much too unsubstantial and rare a foundation for such a superstructure. It is not really true that it was Minette, who strongly influenced Charles in favour of the French alliance. From the beginning of his reign Charles ardently wanted it both for politic and sentimental reasons. It was to be Minette's great task to work tirelessly to achieve it.

With their customary ill fortune just when it seemed that the royal family would enjoy a happy, united Christmas together, fate struck the Stuarts a heavy blow. A few days before Christmas, Princess Mary of Orange (the Princess Royal) suddenly fell ill. She was smitten with smallpox. The doctors in their ignorance advised that she should be bled. Apprehensive and saddened Charles watched by the bedside of Princess Mary in Whitehall Palace while Henrietta Maria fearing that her Henriette might also catch the dreaded disease had her removed to St. James's Palace. Since Charles could not come to see Henriette he wrote to her a loving little note.

47

The kindnesse I have for you will not permitt me to loose
this occasion to conjure you to continue your kindnesse to
a brother that loves you more than he can expresse, which
truth I hope you are persuaded of, as I may expect those
returnes which I shall strive to deserve, deare sister be kinde
to me and be confident that I am intierly yours.

C[13]

As he anxiously watched his eldest sister, moaning and almost
delirious, he must have remembered their happy voyage down
the Rhine together, during his exile. How generous a sister she
had been to her brothers and family! She died on Christmas
Eve at the age of twenty-nine. At least she was spared the pain
of seeing her son William, now an infant, usurp the throne
from her brother James twenty-eight years later, though she
certainly would not have approved of James as a Roman Catholic. The death of this attractive Princess only bound Charles
II closer, if that were possible, to his only surviving sister.

Father Cyprien de Gamaches in his *Mémoires* wrote that the
British observed Christmas, especially in the King's Palaces,
with greater pomp than in any other nation in Europe. It was
the custom to bring a branch of the Glastonbury thorn, which
blossomed on Christmas Eve, to be presented to the King. However, it was a sorrowful royal family party that Christmas, who
spoke in hushed voices, brave and smiling even in their grief.

Monsieur was in despair when he heard of the Princess
Royal's illness and death, and wrote impatient letters to the
Queen begging her to bring back her daughter to France with-
out delay. He sent his *maître d'hôtel* to England for this purpose.

Parliament now determined that a yearly allowance of
£30,000 should be granted the Queen, and the King promised
his mother that she would be allowed an equal amount from
his privy purse. Before leaving for France, Henrietta Maria
who had so far proved inflexible, agreed to recognize the Duke
of York's marriage to Anne Hyde. At a farewell audience in
Whitehall, the Queen received the Duchess of York most gra-

ciously. When the royal family dined in public Father Cyprien was much elated that he was able to read the Latin grace because the English minister stumbled in his attempt to reach his place through the crowds who blocked the doorways.

The Queen and Princess Henriette sailed on 9 January 1661 from Portsmouth in a man-of-war the *London* commanded by the Earl of Sandwich.[14] Madame Marie-Madeleine de La Fayette relates that the Duke of Buckingham at the last moment had obtained Charles II's permission to accompany the royal travellers on their return to France. He was madly in love with the Princess, and could hardly bear to be parted from her.

Queen Henrietta Maria was always very unlucky when travelling by sea. Not only did a violent storm spring up the day after they left Portsmouth, but owing to the negligence of the pilot, the *London* ran aground on the Horse Sand. Then Princess Henrietta fell seriously ill, and for some time it was feared that she had caught smallpox. The Duke of Buckingham became more and more desperate when he believed the Princess's life was in danger, and seemed to those on board like a madman. Madame de La Fayette, who must later have learnt from the Princess herself what had happened during the voyage, relates that Buckingham became so jealous of Edward Montagu, Earl of Sandwich because of his attentions to the Princess that he quarrelled violently with him and wanted to challenge him to a duel. The man-of-war had been damaged while the storm raged and it was found necessary to return to Portsmouth. There the Princess was attended by two of the King's doctors. It may well be that she owed her life to her refusal to allow the physicians to bleed her as had been done during the illnesses of Princess Mary of Orange and the Duke of Gloucester. It was a relief to everybody when it was diagnosed that she was suffering from a severe attack of measles. Her aunt Elizabeth of Bohemia wrote to her eldest son Charles Louis, Elector Palatine: 'My niece Princess Henriette puts me in a new paine, she has the measles on shipboard. They say she is not verie sick with them, but too it was said of my poore nephue the Duke of Gloucester.' Madame de La Fayette relates that the royal travellers were at last able to set sail on 25 January and arrived at Le Havre six days later.

Meanwhile the Duke of Buckingham's behaviour in playing the part of a distracted lover had grown so embarrassing that Queen Henrietta Maria, so as to get rid of him, ordered him forthwith to go to Paris to inform Monsieur of their safe arrival. After remaining several days at Le Havre to recover from the journey, the Queen and the Princess continued their journey towards Paris, escorted by the governor of Normandy, the Duc de Longueville. Instead of staying at Rouen where several cases of smallpox had been reported, the royal party travelled to the Abbey of St. Martin, near Pontoise where they were spendidly entertained by the Queen's almoner and close friend the Abbé Montagu. While the Abbé was showing the Queen and her daughter his treasures, there was the sound of trumpets heralding the arrival of King Louis, Queen Marie-Thérèse and Monsieur, overjoyed to be united with his betrothed. He eagerly listened to every word that fell from her mouth and could hardly take his eyes off her. On the following day Monsieur returned to the Abbey to escort Henriette and her mother to Paris. At St. Denis the cavalcade was joined by King Louis and Queen Marie-Thérèse and they then proceeded in state to the Palais-Royal.

V

Madame's Triumph

A Papal dispensation was necessary for the marriage of Henriette and Philippe because they were first cousins. So, the Queen and her daughter retired for a period to Chaillot to await its arrival. It arrived on 9 March. On that day there died at Vincennes Cardinal Mazarin. Madame de Motteville, who hated him, admitted in her *Mémoires* that 'he looked upon death with such steadfastness that he told M. Joly (his confessor) that he had qualms about not fearing it enough'. His only regret was to have to leave his riches and luxurious way of life. When he was informed by his attendants that a comet, an evil omen, had suddenly appeared in the heavens he remarked with slight irony: 'The Comet does me too much honour.' Shortly before his death, he advised King Louis not to appoint a First Minister, and specially commended Jean-Baptiste Colbert to the King's service, who was to prove an admirable minister. The King, a young man of twenty-three now determined to take power into his own hands. The love of *gloire* and greatness was the consuming motive of his life.

Monsieur became ever more impatient and irritable because the Court went into mourning for a fortnight, and his marriage to the Princess of England was postponed: besides, he was jealous of the Duke of Buckingham, who was paying his betrothed marked attentions. Henriette was amused. She enjoyed his company and his drollery because he was a favourite of her brother's, but now found him too ardent, though she did not take him seriously. In her book *Madame Henriette d'Angleterre*, Madame de La Fayette wrote that the Duke of Buckingham was son of the Duke, who was beheaded. It is inaccurate, for he was in fact assassinated by John Felton in Portsmouth (1629). The First Duke, like his son, had been a creature of impulse. He had the effrontery to attempt to make love to Anne of Austria, then the young Queen of Louis XIII in a garden at Amiens, and scandal had narrowly been averted. Monsieur sulked and complained to his mother, Anne of Austria, of the Second Duke's behaviour. She advised her sister-in-law Queen Henrietta Maria to give her son the King of England a tactful hint that Buckingham should be recalled. Monsieur was unable to conceal his glee when the nobleman left for England, protesting his hopeless, but undying devotion for the Princess.

Although it was Lent and she was still in deep mourning for her brother and sister it was decided that her marriage with Monsieur should take place as soon as possible. On the morning of 30 March 1661 the Princess Henriette of England attended Holy Communion at the Church of St. Eustache the parish church of the Palais-Royal, while Monsieur performed his devotions at St. Germain L'Auxerrois. The betrothal ceremony took place that evening in the great salon of the Palais-Royal in the presence of King Louis and Queen Marie-Thérèse, Queen Henrietta Maria, Queen Anne of Austria, Mademoiselle and other illustrious persons. The bride wore a resplendent dress.

Daniel de Cosnac, Bishop of Valence and Grand Almoner to Monsieur tells us, in his *Mémoires*, that the actual marriage was solemnized in Queen Henrietta's private chapel in the Palais-Royal and that he officiated at the ceremony. There was a great dispute between L'Abbé Montagu Grand Almoner of the Queen of England and himself who should officiate.[1] Henrietta Maria supported the claims of L'Abbé Montagu, while Monsieur contested that Cosnac should perform the ceremony. Cosnac admitted in his *Mémoires* that as the royal couple were being married in the Queen's private chapel, L'Abbé Montagu had a certain claim, but he argued that his episcopal rank gave him a prior claim over a mere abbot.[2] Cosnac, a man of strong personality, was successful in gaining his point, and officiated in Henrietta Maria's chapel. Among those present was the Earl of St. Albans, the British Ambassador, who represented King Charles II.

After her marriage to Monsieur, Princess Henriette was known as Madame at the French Court. It was natural for Monsieur, a few days after his wedding to take his bride to his own residence at the Tuileries where he would be freed of the presence of his mother-in-law the Queen of England, but the young Princess not yet seventeen cried bitterly at the separation from her mother, for she had never been separated from her since her escape to France with Lady Morton in her infancy.

Monsieur had seemed passionately in love with the Princess before marriage and it had thrived during her absence in England. It is certainly true that she had succeeded in arousing a boy's love in him which attained its height when they were apart from one another. Madame de La Fayette, who knew Philippe intimately, wrote that the miracle of inflaming the heart of this prince was not given to any woman upon earth. Mademoiselle, who had few illusions about Philippe's character, thought that he only cared for his own beauty and his clothes, and that he was quite unable to distinguish himself by noble actions or to take a leading part among men. That is not quite fair, for Monsieur showed that he possessed courage on active service. It was his brother the King, who wanted to keep him in the background, jealous that Monsieur might reveal that he was of finer mettle. Philippe did not only care for himself. It is evident that he later truly loved his minion the Chevalier Philippe de Loraine, who was to cause Madame such misery. Monsieur's biographer Philippe Erlanger wrote that he loved this self-seeking, despicable man for thirty years, the only creature capable of giving consolation to Monsieur in his misery. Monsieur was abnormal, and it could not be expected that a young princess not yet seventeen would understand or condole with his peculiarities. He himself admitted in his later life that after the first fortnight of his married life he had never

loved his wife. He was, perhaps, to be pitied rather than condemned.

Monsieur might indeed take pride in wooing Henriette when
nobody else desired her, but the little despised girl had blossomed into an enchanting Princess, a charming conversational-
ist, graceful in her movements, her mind vigorous and culti-
vated, her sentiments great and noble. She possessed the rare
gift of pleasing almost everybody. A Courtier wrote of her:
'When she speaks to you, she seems to ask for your heart at
once, however trifling are the words that she has to say.' She
was very witty, but her wit was never unkind.

> Never [wrote L'Abbé de Choisy, a contemporary] has
> France had a Princess as attractive as Henriette d'Angleterre
> when she became the wife of Monsieur. . . . Her whole person
> seemed full of charm. You felt interested in her, you loved
> her without being able to help yourself. . . .[3]

He added that Henriette d'Angleterre had all the talent necessary for conducting important affairs, had this been required
of her. At the court of the young King in those days, pleasure
was the order of the day and to be charming was enough.

Young King Louis himself was captivated by his sister-in-
law's charm and vivacity, and declared aloud that he must have
been the most unjust of men, not to think Madame the fairest
and best of women. She certainly would have been a more suitable Queen for him than Marie-Thérèse, although Louis as a
young man was incapable of fidelity for long to any woman.
With her pride as Princess of England, Madame would have
resented his infidelities, even if they were expected of a Prince
in those days.

The personality of Madame glowed all the stronger in com-
parison with the dull and insipid mentality of Marie-Thérèse.
The Queen was a slave to Spanish etiquette, even asking the
Court Chamberlain in Madrid for permission to kiss her father
Philip IV.[4] If she had enjoyed intercourse with her husband,
she would take a childish pleasure in clapping her hands the

following morning in public before the courtiers. She was extremely greedy, and liked to reserve the most tasty dishes for herself alone. She only took occasional exercise, and was inclined to be lethargic and melancholy. She liked gambling at cards, and was encouraged to do so by the courtiers, for she invariably lost. Despite her heavy Spanish piety and her ignorance, Marie-Thérèse possessed a kind heart.[4] She was extremely fond of Louis and was very jealous of his mistresses. Such a woman was incapable of playing the part of Queen at the brilliant Court of Louis XIV, for she had no gifts of conversation or repartee, and felt completely inadequate if she had to preside at state receptions or banquets.

Consequently many of the Queen's duties devolved on Madame, and she sometimes presided at the reception of foreign ambassadors. On Maundy Thursday, she represented the Queen in the traditional ceremony of washing the feet of the poor, in the hall of the Louvre.

With the possible exception of Madame's aunt Elizabeth of Bohemia, the 'Queen of Hearts', none of the Princesses of the House of Stuart had a greater gift or what may be described as a genius for friendship than Henriette D'Angleterre. Her most intimate friend throughout her brief life was Marie-Madeleine Pioche de La Vergne Madame de La Fayette, who had been born in Paris in 1634. She was a devoted friend of Madame de Sévigné, and was often a favoured guest at the Hotel Rambouillet. Madame de La Fayette's husband, who had never counted much in her life, died early leaving her a widow with two children. She was a clever novelist with a special predilection for the Court of the Valois, so that she liked to place the action of her novels during this period. When Madame first became friendly with her, she had already published her first romance, La Princesse de Montpensier, but one of her best works La Princesse de Clèves did not see the light of day until after the Princess's death. To English readers she is, perhaps, best known for her biography of Madame Henriette D'Angleterre.

Another of Madame's intimate friends in those early years was Marguerite de La Trémouille, niece of the French-born Countess of Derby, who had praised Henriette so highly during her visit to England. It was a loss to Madame when Marguerite married a German Prince and was obliged to leave France for Germany. Another close friend was Elizabeth-Angélique de Montmorency-Bouteville, Duchess de Châtillon, a link between Charles II and his sister because she was an old flame of the King's during his exile. She had even boasted to Mademoiselle that she might one day become Queen of England. Henriette and Charles referred to her in their letters by a pet name Bablon. When she married a German Duke three years later, Charles in his characteristic way wrote that he was sorry that she was exchanging France for Germany. However, the resourceful lady now known as Madame de Meckelbourg made it a condition of her marriage that she should be allowed to return to France as often and for as long as she wished.

When the King and Queen departed for Fontainebleau during the spring (1661), Monsieur and Madame remained at the Tuileries in Paris for a few weeks longer where they were surrounded by a brilliant Court. Madame, not yet seventeen, would daily drive in her coach accompanied by her ladies to the Cours de La Reine, a pleasant avenue on the Seine originally laid out by the disagreeable Queen of Henri IV, Marie de Medicis. There was plenty of gaiety in the evening, plays, music, and dancing. Madame was universally admired, and even her husband was proud of her, though already a little envious of her success. Everybody was impressed by her sensitive and delicate taste for books, and it was now clearly perceived that her education in private was a great advantage to her. Some regretted that she was not Queen of France, although by way of compensation she desired to reign in the hearts of all men.

After paying a visit to her mother Queen Henrietta at Colombes during May, Monsieur and Madame continued their journey to St. Cloud, that 'palais de délices' as her favourite home was called.

With all his faults Monsieur had excellent taste, and the palais was exquisitely furnished and decorated with objets d'art and beautiful things. The most celebrated architects of the Court of Louis XIV such as Lepante and Girard had been employed to enlarge and embellish the palace, while Le Nôtre, greatest of landscape gardeners and formerly in the employ of Fouquet, King Louis's minister designed the park and gardens. Then there was the young architect, Jules Hardouin Mansart, later like Le Nôtre so closely associated with Versailles, who laid out the lovely cascades and Jets d'eau at St. Cloud. From the terraces there were wonderful views of the Seine and the distant Paris. There were burbling brooks, enchanting the ear with the sweetness of their music, and bosky places to retreat to. Madame's favourite part of the gardens was near to the Grande Cascade. There she later loved to sit with Madame de Fayette or one of her other friends on beautiful summer evenings talking about the latest play, about literature, or merely contemplating the scene and taking pleasure in the delicious scents. It was the place where she was destined to experience the happiest and most desolate periods in her brief life.

There is a letter from King Louis revealing that he was already very attracted to his young sister-in-law. He wrote from Fontainebleau on a Friday:

> If I wish myself at Saint-Cloud it is not because of its grottoes or the freshness of its foliage. Here we have gardens fair enough to console us, but the company which is there now, is so good that I find myself furiously tempted to go there, and if I did not expect to see you here tomorrow, I do not know what I should do, and could not help making a journey to see you ... give my best love to my brother.[5]

On the following day Monsieur and Madame left for the Palace of Fontainebleau to join the French Court. There on the edge of the celebrated forest the spirit of François I seems to linger, particularly in its exquisite Renaissance rooms. There this sly man made love to his mistresses, and enjoyed the hunting in the surrounding forest. Henri IV, one of France's greatest kings, had jousted and revelled here through the long summer days. Louis XIII had been born at Fontainebleau and here too, Princess Henriette's great-grandmother Mary Queen of Scots had enjoyed the happiest days of her tragic life. How bitter it was for her to have to leave France!

Now an enchanting Princess came to Fontainebleau, to dazzle the French Court with the brilliance of her quick wit, her ability to enjoy to the utmost the fugitive summer days that fled too quickly. On state occasions nobody was more royal than Madame, but on informal occasions she preferred to be unconventional and she was to be criticised for this. To be the centre of attraction, to be the cherished companion of Le Roi Soleil himself, what a sweet balm for the spirit of this girl just seventeen, so neglected during her early days in France. Is it a crime to be a little frivolous when one is young and to throw discretion to the winds?

Madame, too, in the flush of her first beauty, realized that the King, who despised her as a little girl now entertained very different feelings for her. Louis sought her company and encouraged his sister-in-law to take a leading part in organizing the entertainments, for Marie-Thérèse seemed incapable of playing her part as his Queen.

At Fontainebleau the King and Queen occupied the State apartments situated on the left side of the Court in the oval. On the same side, in the pavilion called 'the princes' at the entrance to the same courtyard were Monsieur and Madame's apartments[6] and her maids of honour also stayed here.

During the long reign of Louis XIV never was there a summer like the summer of 1661. Freed from tiresome restrictions, no longer under the domination of his mother and Cardinal Mazarin dead, Louis was his own master. He had not yet attained his twenty-third birthday and gloried in the vigour of his manhood. He was at his best, his mind full of noble schemes and aspirations before the stifling and dull routine of Versailles had settled inexorably on him. His ambition was to transform his father's hunting lodge at Versailles into a resplendent palace. He never neglected state affairs, for he spent the mornings closeted with his ministers and used to write despatches to his foreign ambassadors in his own hand. For the rest of the day Louis enjoyed himself, revelling in the beauty of sunlight and shade in the Hermitage de Franchard. He sat in the cool forest surrounded by his courtiers as the royal servants prepared the dainty collations. Then later in the evening embarking with Madame and other favoured royal guests on the waters of the canal while the strains of Lulli's exquisite violins floated to them, the moonlight bathing the river in its soft radiance.

As for Madame she revelled in the sense of freedom from restraint. Throughout her short life she loved bathing and there were many hot days that June when Madame attended by ladies of the Court would be driven in her carriage because of the heat through the forest glades to some favourite stream to bathe. She was an expert horsewoman, and we can visualize her returning from these expeditions, wearing a gold-laced dress and a gay plume in her hat, happy to indulge in simple pleasures and radiant in the knowledge that the King greatly admired her. Together with Louis she took the leading part in the hunting expeditions and solitary moonlight walks with the King far into the night in the cool depths of the forest.

King Louis and Madame took the leading parts in a ballet by Benserade. It reminded her of her first public appearance at the age of nine when she had spoken his verses. In another ballet in which the dances were on horseback to the light of torches, the King and Madame again played the principal roles. Everybody noticed Louis's marked attachment to the Princess.

Fontainebleau was very gay that June. On the 14th there was an open-air ball, given by the Duke of Beaufort, followed nine evenings later by an entertainment organized by the Duc de St. Aignan, a confidant of the King's. Monsieur and Madame were the hosts at a ball, and there was a torchlight procession after a dance when the Duc D'Enghien was the host.

In the whirl of excitement produced by all this gaiety, it is unlikely that Madame had paused to consider the true nature of her feelings towards her brother-in-law. That she found the young Louis very attractive is certain, but it is less easy to accept that there was a great romance between Louis and the Princess. Princess Henriette evoked those joyous days when later discuss-' ing the episode in her life with Madame de La Fayette. As this lady delicately put it: 'She did not think that the King pleased her save as a brother-in-law, though it may be that he pleased her more.'

Madame de La Fayette relates in her *Histoire de Madame Henriette* that the Queen-Mother Anne of Austria disapproved of Louis's attachment to Madame. Madame de Motteville, the intimate friend of Anne of Austria wrote that the Queen took the opportunity of warning her daughter-in-law against too frequent walks with the King in the Forest of Fontainebleau. Besides, her health could be adversely affected by the hunting parties and constant attendance at balls.[7] 'Youth does not lend itself easily to reason', wrote Madame de Motteville philosophically. The Princess only laughed at her mother-in-law's fears, disregarded her advice and repeated what she had said to the King. Anne of Austria, who had so petted the Princess Henriette when a little girl, grew very indignant. She complained that owing to Madame's influence Louis was neglecting his wife and his mother.

As for Monsieur, he had first preened himself on his cleverness in appreciating Princess Henriette when his brother had despised her. He had been proud of his young wife. Now he felt increasing resentment—and it was natural for him to have such sentiments. What really hurt him was not so much jealousy at his wife's behaviour, but anger that Madame was acquiring too great influence over his brother the King. Louis neglected him in seeking the companionship of his wife. Spoilt boys run to their mothers and Monsieur complained to the Queen-Mother about Madame. Anne of Austria now implored her sister-in-law Queen Henrietta to speak seriously to her daughter. The Queen of England from Colombes decided to write to her old friend Madame de Motteville. 'You have with you my other little self (*un autre petit moi-même*)—who loves you well I can assure you—I beg of you remain her friend.' It was a delicate way of putting it, but Madame de Motteville's tactful remonstrances were no more heeded than those of the Queen-Mother of France.

It was during these evanescent days that the rising dramatist Molière's witty comedy *École des Maris* was performed for the first time. Actually it took place at a splendid fête given by Nicolas Fouquet, Surintendant des Finances at his lovely house at Vaux. Molière had already shown promise of a comic genius and his troupe had often performed in the theatre of the Palais-Royal. Molière was the former protége of the Prince de Conti, who had recommended him to Monsieur. In his turn Monsieur presented Molière to the King, who after seeing a performance of *Les Précieuses Ridicules* said, though he had a rudimentary knowledge of literature: 'This man Molière suits me, he is amusing and clearsighted.' It was Madame, however, who showed most insight and appreciation of Molière's plays, bestowing on him her generous patronage and giving him a sympathy all the more needed when a few of his contemporaries were savagely criticising him.

Madame's triumph, her brief reign, culminated in the exquisite *Ballet des Saisons* played before the Queen and the whole Court at Fontainebleau on 23 July. Madame played the part of Diana, queen and huntress, while Louis paid homage to her as Spring. Nobody could conceive a more wonderful setting; the stage erected on a grassy bank on the edge of the lake, and the avenue of trees illuminated with thousands of torches, a fiery glow lighting the waters. The curtain rose and Madame appeared, wearing the silver crescent on her brow, and armed with bow and arrow. She was attended by ten of the most beautiful ladies of the Court, including Frances Stuart, who was later to cause Charles II such anguish in Whitehall. Louise de la Vallière attended Madame as did Madame de Monaco, a sister of the Comte de Guiche. Monsieur, too, had his part in this ballet, and appeared with the Comte de Guiche still his favourite. The ballet ended with King Louis sinking graciously on his knees to offer homage to Madame, and calling her Queen of Beauty.

Queen Marie-Thérèse, who was of a jealous temperament, now constantly complained to her husband that he preferred Madame's society to her own. No wonder she bored Louis. She was short almost like a dwarf, though she was far from ugly. She was fond of her dogs and dwarfs. She never really acquired a taste for French food, preferring clove-scented chocolate from Mexico and garlic stews with nutmegs and capsicums.[8] Her Spanish piety got on his nerves.

It was necessary for Madame and Louis to put an end to the malicious stories about their friendship. One day at Fontainebleau when discussing the matter they concocted a plot that Louis should pretend to make love to one of the ladies of the Court. At first Mlle. de Pons—a girl of doubtful virtue—and Mlle. de Chimerault, another coquette, were chosen, and then Henriette thought of her own maid of honour Louise de La Vallière, who was about three months younger than her.[9] Madame de La Fayette describes Louise as 'fort jolie, fort douce, et fort naive'. She was fair, very pretty and rather tall, with sparkling blue eyes, and had a slight limp. La Fontaine's lines

*Et la grâce, plus belle
encore que la beauté*

aptly describe her. Unlike many of the girls at Court, she had been bred in the country. Born at Tours, she had lived much at Orléans and Blois. Her fortune might be meagre, but she came of a good family. She rode a horse beautifully, an accomplishment which must have appealed to Louis. She was unusually shy and romantic, and it may well be that she had already fallen in love with the King before he noticed her some time during June. During that enchanting summer several admirers had already courted her, including the Comte de Guiche. It is evident that Louise fell desperately in love with the King, and he in his turn perceiving this and flattered by her spontaneous devotion soon became enamoured of her. His feigned passion became a reality. In the wild and romantic setting of Fontainebleau they rode together or walked in the beech woods. On one occasion the soft, delicious rain began to fall and the King sheltered her with his hat.

When she realized that Louis had really become attached to Louise de La Vallière, her insignificant maid of honour, Madame was very piqued. No young woman—and Henriette was barely seventeen—likes her cavalier to be taken from her. It is difficult to analyse her feelings, but she felt a sense of uneasiness. It did not amount to acute jealousy, but she certainly resented that Louis should be paying ardent court to her maid of honour. She regretted ever suggesting that the King should pretend to make love to Mlle. de La Vallière. She was subtly aware that after the King visited her in her carriage during the evenings he went straight to La Vallière's carriage to whisper soft words to his new love in the enfolding darkness.

VI

Intrigues and Love Affairs

Princess Henriette and the Duke of Buckingham were conversing one day in the ship bearing them to Le Havre from Portsmouth while a howling storm raged outside. It is said that Buckingham wagered with her a pair of gloves that the first person to fall in love with her after marriage would be Armand de Gramont Comte de Guiche. This extremely handsome and gallant courtier and soldier had often appeared with Madame during the summer (1661) in the ballets and masquerades at Fontainebleau. They often sang and danced together. He was then twenty-four, a man who had married against his own inclinations three years before to Marguerite Louise Suzanne de Béthune, daughter of the Duke of Sully. He was very attractive to women.

Madame de La Fayette describes de Guiche as '*galant, hardi, brave, rempli de grandeur et d'élevation*'. De Guiche[1] had a good figure, large intelligent eyes and an interesting, pale face. His main defects were his undeniable vanity, and his manner was sometimes disdainful, even insolent. Madame de Sévigné said that there was a supernatural air about him, so that he bore no resemblance to the ordinary run of men. He was a hero of romance and might have sprung from a poem by Byron. His father was the respected and honourable Maréchal de Gramont much liked by Louis XIV, his uncle the celebrated Chevalier de Gramont, his sister the beautiful Princess de Monaco a close friend of Madame's, while his aunt was Madame de Saint-Chaumont, later to be appointed Governess to Madame's children.

So long as King Louis was overwhelming Madame with his

attentions, de Guiche had not ventured to avow his passion. Only after Louis became enamoured of Mlle. de La Vallière did he become bolder and more resolute. De Guiche had been a favourite of Monsieur, very different from the mincing, pretty boys, who swarmed about Monsieur, but the older man had little respect for the King's brother, for on one occasion he had even kicked him on the bottom, whilst dancing, according to La Grande Mademoiselle. During the summer (1661) the courtiers observed an ardent look in his eyes when he was with Madame.

Madame de La Fayette relates that one day when he was rehearsing a scene in the Ballets des Saisons he asked Madame if nothing had ever touched her. She made some merry retort, and de Guiche went away murmuring that he was in great peril. Monsieur now became more and more suspicious and sulky. He blamed his wife for depriving him of his favourite's friendship. Discord spread in Monsieur's household. The passion of the Comte de Guiche for Madame soon became the talk of the French Court.

Princess Henriette was only seventeen. She was by temperament a coquette, a great flirt, but it may well be that she was at first unaware of de Guiche's secret adoration of her. She was flattered, but found him slightly absurd. Madame wanted to be loved and admired but despite herself she played havoc with the hearts of men, while she captivated their minds. Certainly the affair with Madame—and it is extremely unlikely that de Guiche ever enjoyed complete physical intimacy with her—was to cause them both deep distress and unhappiness. It was to harm her image at King Louis's Court. Madame as she matured was not of a passionate nature, nor did her delicate health allow it. So great was her charm, her magnetism, that when she talked to men she seemed to ask for their hearts. De Guiche himself admitted: 'She had a way of speaking to anyone which seemed to ask for their love, however trivial were the words.'

The Marquis de la Fare, who knew her well, believed that

she was entirely virtuous, though she certainly flirted with de Guiche outrageously. On one occasion de Guiche mentioned to her that he was the victim of a hopeless passion, and he described the lady in such glowing terms that she could scarcely remain unaware that he alluded to her. She was later to grow extremely fond of de Guiche. In her affairs of the heart she was capable of acting indiscreetly without taking ordinary precautions. However, when Henriette first learnt that Armand de Guiche had openly confessed his passion for her, she told his sister Madame de Monaco to tell her brother not to appear again in her presence and refused to read one of his letters. Later she relented. It was a source of satisfaction to the young princess that she had an acknowledged adorer: a subtle revenge for Louis's love affair with Louise de La Vallière.

One of the most lavish fêtes ever to be given was one in which Nicolas Fouquet, Superintendent of the Finances, was the host at his country estate at Vaux-Le-Vicomte, thirty miles southeast of Paris. It was on 17 August that King Louis and the whole French Court went over to Vaux. Madame in whose honour the fête was given, had been ill and was carried in a litter by two running footmen, who bore the poles in their hands. For some time Louis had suspected, not without reason, that Fouquet had acquired his great wealth by dishonest means. He had mismanaged the nation's finances. The King also disliked Fouquet on personal grounds because he had made insulting proposals to Louise de La Vallière. She had complained to the King. He had offered her 20,000 pistoles (£70,000) if she were to speak well of him to the King. The Abbé de Choisy wrote that Fouquet the minister, who was soon to be disgraced by Louis XIV, dared to lift his eyes to Mlle. de La Vallière. This conceited man with flashing dark eyes and attractive long eyelashes fancied himself as a ladies' man.

After a performance of Molière's new comedy *Les Fachêux* (The Bores) in an open-air theatre, there was a magnificent display of fireworks. La Fontaine described the lovely scene. The boat shaped like a whale, which glided up and down the canal letting off more fireworks, the thousands of rockets rising and falling in the air as Louis went back to the house, the delicious supper served to the music of twenty-four violins, so beloved by the King of France.

To Madame, compelled that summer night to remain in her litter, it seemed that her influence with the King was on the wane, and that La Vallière's was in the ascendant. As she marvelled at the beauty of the scene, she was conscious of the tension all around, the mysterious whispers, the cries of delight as the sparks of the fireworks vanished in the water. She sensed the helpless anger of the King, who felt like arresting Fouquet in his own house had he not been dissuaded by his mother Anne of Austria. The insolence of the man! It made the King angry to see Fouquet's arms, a squirrel with the motto: *'Quo non ascendans?'* on every wall. Less than a month later, Fouquet was arrested at Nantes, and tried in the arsenal on charges of malversation and treason. He was sentenced to life imprisonment in the fortress of Pignerol. Truly, Louis was now his own master, and he instructed Colbert to reform the finances in the Kingdom.

Exhausted by the constant strain of having to appear at fêtes, and other activities, Madame's health was in a precarious state during the winter (1661–2). She was pregnant, suffered from an irritating cough, and was compelled to take opium, according to Mademoiselle, in order to sleep. When William Lord Crofts of Saxham, a gentleman of Charles II's Bedchamber returned to London after congratulating the King and Queen of France on the birth of a Dauphin he gave his master an alarming report about his sister's health. Writing to her from Whitehall on 16 December Charles begs her: 'for God's sake my dearest sister have a care of your selfe and I believe that I am more concerned in your health than I am in my owne'. . . . She had told him she longed to see him in Dunkirk the following summer, and he shared that longing.

which you may easily beleeve is a very welcome proposition to me . . . I shall be very impatient till I have the happiness to see ma chère Minete againe, I am very glad to finde that the K. of France does still continue his confidence and kindness to you, which I am so sensible of, that if I had no other reason to grounde my kindnesse to him by that he may be most assumed of my friendship as long as I live. . . . I do intend to write to you very often in English that you may not quite forgett it.

The letter is endorsed 'For my dearest Sister'.

It is significant because it shows the importance Charles early attached to his relations with King Louis and that he wanted his sister as his agent very often to represent his views to the French King.

It is evident that Minette's ardent hope to see her brother in Dunkirk was to be frustrated, for her letter in the Lambeth Palace Collection (written on 22 July 1662) alludes to a courier bringing her, *'la plus méchante nouvelle'*.[2] 'Those in the highest quarters', she wrote to her brother, 'were as pleased as I was miserable.' There were French politicians who resented that she was so frequently in communication with her brother. It is the only occasion when she calls herself *'votre pauvre Minete'*.

Charles's letters to his sister reveal his real pride in England's naval supremacy and he was consistent at least in his determination to maintain it. King Louis objected to the salute at sea it was customary for English men-of-war to insist on from the ships of all other nations. In those early days France's fleet was negligible, though it was later to become more powerful. Louis, however, in his desire for aggrandisement wanted to claim this privilege for himself. Evidently he communicated his views on this delicate subject to Madame. Those who so glibly accuse Charles II of lack of patriotism, might well study the King's letter (23 December 1661) to Madame.

I extremely wonder at that which you invite me, [he told her] for certainly never any ships refused to strike there Pavilion when they mett any ships belonging to the Crowne of England. . . .

Intrigues and Love Affairs

The dispute was to remain a bone of contention for many years between the two nations. When he received the new French Ambassador, The Comte d'Estrades, at his first audience, King Charles firmly upheld his views, saying that he would rather lose his crown than to abandon the salute at sea.[3] Unfortunately the letter from Madame in which she alluded to this affair has been lost.

During this period the marriage of Charles II and the Infanta Catherine of Portugal was being negotiated, and the French King certainly helped to effect it. The French diplomat Ruvigni once wrote to Cardinal Mazarin that the King had 'an unconquerable aversion for Northern women'.[4] Nor did German princesses tempt him, for he described them as dull and foggy. Among the girls appointed to the position of maid of honour in the Queen of England's household was the exquisite Frances Stuart, then aged fifteen, a friend of Madame's, for Frances had been brought up in the household of Queen Henrietta Maria. She was the elder daughter of an exiled cavalier, the Honourable Walter Stuart, a younger son of the First Lord Blantyr.

Minette described Frances to her brother in a letter written in Paris to Charles as '*La plus jolie fille du monde*',[5] little realizing the havoc Frances would later create in her brother's capacious heart. She was very sorry to lose her, for Frances was both loyal and intelligent.

Paris was very gay that winter. Madame had recovered from her illness and reclining on her sofa she received visitors from early morning until late at night. Plays were performed in her apartments at the Tuileries. Louis often came there, dominated by his passion for Louise de La Vallière. Madame thought it very unfair that her mother-in-law and Queen Marie Thérèse should blame her for the King's constant attendance. She wanted if possible to find an excuse for Louise to leave her household.

The Court abounded with intrigues. There were evil-minded people only too ready to stir up trouble between Madame and

Monsieur and King Louis and Louise de La Vallière. Mademoiselle de Montalais, for instance, was not so much evil-minded, but she was a born mischief-maker and intrigante. She was daughter of Pierre Seigneur de Montalais and of Réné Le Clerc de Soutré and a childhood friend of Louise de La Vallière's. That did not deter her from betraying Louise's naïve confidences. King Louis was aware that Anne-Constance de Montalais had been one of Nicolas Fouquet's lady friends and in that capacity had spied on the King for that self-seeking politician, so he forbade his mistress to have anything more to do with Anne-Constance. Louise, however, continued to see her, for she was also one of Madame's maids-of-honour.

Mlle. de Montalais enjoyed acting as go-between in Madame's affair with de Guiche. That nobleman was so much in love with Madame that he wrote her three or four letters a day, and Montalais would toss them into Madame's litter for her mistress to read. It was indiscreet and dangerous for Madame to confide in this girl, but she was not yet eighteen and could hardly be expected to have the discretion of an older woman. The Princess liked excitement, but she was playing with fire when she allowed de Guiche stolen interviews in her apartments. On one occasion the Comte in the guise of a fortune-teller, according to Madame de La Fayette's account, managed to penetrate Madame's apartments, much to her amusement. Anne-Constance resorted to many subterfuges. It was folly on the Princess's part to allow these visits, but she was almost certainly never unfaithful to Monsieur.

'Every single lady at Court has the ambition to become the King's mistress,' wrote an Italian contemporary Primi Visconti. And many married ladies as well one might add. Olympia Mancini Comtesse de Soissons who had once aroused the adolescent love of Louis XIV and possibly been his mistress, hated Louise de La Vallière and wished to compass her downfall. She was possessive by nature, especially in her relations with the King of France and wanted to retain her influence with him. She was a sophisticated lady and as Superintendent of the Queen's household it was all too easy for her to have access to Marie Thérèse's apartments. Her salon at the Tuileries in Paris was the centre of Court intrigue. There she would give sumptuous parties. Celebrated for her love affairs, she was during the winter (1661–2) the mistress of that sinister Courtier François René du Bec Crespin, Marquis de Vardes, a gentleman of the Bedchamber of Louis XIV. Vardes was very tall and would have been handsome except for his too massive jaw. His head was magnificent, leonine in its great wig. He possessed the restlessness of a prowling lion and his character was treacherous and despicable. Olympia and Vardes conspired to ruin Louise de La Vallière by composing an anonymous letter, translated into Spanish, in which they informed Queen Marie-Thérèse of the King's love for Mlle. de La Vallière. An extract read:

> It is for you to consider whether you can tolerate the thought of the King in the arms of another, or if you will put an end to a situation so humiliating to your dignity.

Fortunately, it fell into the hands of the Queen's Spanish lady-in-waiting, Dona Molina, who very prudently handed the letter to Anne of Austria. She instructed Dona Molina to give it to the King, who failed to discover the author of the letter. The Marquis de Vardes, who was irresistible to most women, later aspired to make Madame his mistress, and for a time she gave him her friendship until she perceived his real character.

King Louis's love for his mistress was at its height. There was grave scandal at Court. Anne of Austria, deeply anxious and fearing that the Queen's health would be affected, remonstrated with her son, not without effect.

One day Madame told her young maid-of-honour that she must leave her service, and Louise weeping bitterly fled to a convent near St. Cloud. After diligent inquiry Louis discovered where Louise had taken refuge and rode forthwith to the Convent to beg her to return with him to the Tuileries. Louis begged Madame to take her maid-of-honour back into her service, and the Princess, though with extreme reluctance, for she was very proud, agreed to do so. However, she could not refrain from saying to the King, that in future she would consider La Vallière his property *'une fille-à-vous'*.

Just before giving birth to her elder daughter on 27 March 1662, Henriette accompanied her mother-in-law to a thanksgiving service at Val-de-Grâce. Then three days later she was present with Queen Marie-Thérèse when they gave the Spanish Ambassador an audience. Madame was in an over-wrought state when she prematurely gave birth to her infant daughter in the Palais-Royal. She is supposed to have heartlessly exclaimed: 'Then throw her into the river!' Her mother-in-law was deeply shocked and told the Duchess of Orléans that her baby daughter might yet become Queen by marrying the Dauphin only a few months older than her. The infant was christened Marie-Louise, and many years latter married the wretched weakling Charles II of Spain, who was devoted to her. Madame was young and it was thought highly probable that she would give birth to a son. Everybody knew that Monsieur was abnormal sexually, but he was at least capable of having children.

Vardes pretended to be a friend of the Comte de Guiche, but in reality he wanted to ruin him. He wished to supplant him with Madame. He went to see the young man's father the Maréchal de Gramont, and after complaining that de Guiche had broken his promise to the King that he would not see Madame, begged the Maréchal to ask for the Command of the Nancy garrison for his son. De Gramont nothing loath to get rid of his troublesome son, welcomed the proposal. In his interview with Madame the treacherous Vardes told her that de Guiche had begged the Nancy post from the King. Bussy-Rabatin, who was a friend of Madame's tells us[6] how Madame granted de Guiche a final secret interview. As they were talking, they heard Monsieur's footstep on the stone floor ascending the stairs. Very adroitly the resourceful Montalais who was present pushed de Guiche into a vast chimney. Monsieur room and began to eat an orange—he was very fond of sweets and fruit—and he was about to throw the peel into the grate when Montalais forestalled him by saying ever so sweetly, 'Oh, Monsieur, are you going to throw away that lovely peel when you know I am so fond of it; please give it to me,' and Montalais swallowed the peel in one mouthful.

Unfortunately another of Madame's maids-of-honour Mlle. d'Artigny, who hated de Guiche, went to Queen Anne of Austria's apartments with her story that de Guiche was in Madame's apartments. Monsieur was informed, but he acted with more sense than usual. Although he complained to his mother-in-law Queen Henrietta Maria, he accepted his wife's story that Montalais had been present throughout the interview. Montalais lost her post, but she took with her some of Madame's correspondence, and later handed it over to her lover, an unscrupulous blackguard named Malicorne. As for Mlle. d'Artigny it was soon apparent that she was enceinte, although a single lady. Madame not unnaturally disliked her for her disloyalty and disapproved of her morals. She declared her intention to dismiss her. Madame de La Fayette relates that Mlle. d'Artigny begged her friend Louise de La Vallière to appeal to the King. Louis agreed to discuss the matter with his sister-in-law but Madame de La Fayette relates that 'the affair made some noise, and even gave rise to some discord between the King and Madame'. It was the Marquis de Vardes, who finally succeeded in persuading Madame to retain d'Artigny.

On 23 May 1662 King Charles wrote to his sister from Portsmouth, announcing his marriage to Catherine of Braganza. For a short time Charles's Portuguese Queen enjoyed idyllic happiness with her husband at Hampton Court. Then Charles II dominated by his physical passion for his mistress, the rapacious Lady Castlemaine, announced his intention of making her Lady of the Bedchamber to his wife. Catherine was perfectly right in protesting against this cruel and arbitrary decision. There were bitter recriminations, but Catherine, who already loved the King, was forced to agree to it. It is not possible to defend Charles's attitude in this matter, goaded as he undoubtedly was by the nagging of his tempestuous favourite. Lord Clarendon who hated 'The Lady' as he called her, protested and consequently incurred Charles's displeasure.

Madame refers to the affair in a letter. It is not true that she so admired her brother that she was incapable occasionally of criticizing him. She clearly thought that he was in the wrong, and she delicately reproves him. It is a classic example of her exquisite tact.

> You tell me [she wrote] that someone has spoken maliciously about a person near to the Queen (Lady Castlemaine) your wife. Alas! How can one possibly say such things? I who know your innocence marvel at it. But jesting apart I pray you tell me how the Queen takes this. It is said here that she is grieved beyond measure [*une douleur sans pareille*] and to speak frankly I think it is with reason. As for that kind of thing, there is trouble enough here, not through the Queen as with you, but through the mistresses. Adieu! I am more your servant than anyone in the world.[7]

Madame is alluding to King Louis's pursuit of Mlle. de La Motte Houdancourt, one of his queen's maids-of-honour during the summer of 1662. For a time Louise de La Vallière was very jealous and full of despair Louis soon discovered that the artful lady's letters were carefully composed by friends of the Comtesse de Soissons. Madame de La Fayette relates that Louis was so angry that he refused to have anything more to do with La Motte Houdancourt. It was in the following year that Olympia Mancini, Comtesse de Soissons gave birth to an infant son, Prince Eugen of Savoy, destined to be a soldier of genius.

When Queen Henrietta Maria was about to depart for England to visit Charles at the end of July 1662, La Grande Mademoiselle accompanied her aunt to Saint Denis. The Queen remarked, according to La Grande Mademoiselle: 'I will never forgive you the injury you have done my son in not wishing to marry him, I assure you that you would have been extremely happy.' Bearing in mind Mademoiselle's haughty tactless disposition there is little doubt that the royal couple would have been miserable. Father Cyprien went with his royal mistress, though he was loath to leave Madame.

Charles refers to his mother in his letter of 8 September to Minette.

> I assure you there is nothing I love so well as my dearest Minette [he wrote] ... the truth is never any children had so good a mother as we have, and you and I shall never have any dispute but only who loves her best and in that I will never yield to you.

Though they had frequently quarrelled in France, Charles was now fully reconciled to his mother. Madame had written to her mother about her quarrel with the King of France. It is very unfortunate that the letter has been lost or destroyed, because it would have given more details about the Mademoiselle d'Artigny affair. 'You were much in the right,' Charles assured her, 'he (Louis) has so much ingenuity not to do what he did.' Charles also alludes in his delightful way to the Chevalier de Gramont, brother of Madame de St. Chaumont, who had incurred the King of France's displeasure by his amorous intrigues. He was now in England, and Charles was doing everything possible to fine him a rich wife.

Madame was always ready to oblige a friend, and on 20 November 1662 we find her writing to her brother about his old flame 'Bablon', Elizabeth-Angélique de Montmorency Bouteville, Duchesse de Châtillon.[8] The bearer of this letter was the Comte de Vivonne, First gentleman of the Bedchamber to Louis XIV. He was a brother of Mademoiselle de Tonnay-Charente, afterwards Madame de Montespan, Louis XIV's celebrated mistress. It is probable that 'Bablon' was asking Charles II for some trading monopoly or privilege, but we do not know for certain.

When a new French Ambassador the Comte de Cominges was about to leave for London during December 1662,

Madame entrusted him with a letter to her brother. The appointment of Gaston Jean Baptiste Comte de Cominges to this important post was not a particularly sagacious one on the part of King Louis, for Cominges, though an able man, was of a blunt, truculent temper and his accomplishments did not include a gift for foreign languages. He was a soldier by profession rather than a diplomat. Furthermore, Charles II personally disliked him. Although Cominges had been sent for the express purpose of negotiating a close alliance between France and England he soon perceived that the English people were hostile to such a project.

On one occasion, however, he accompanied Charles II to Portsmouth to view the British fleet. The ambassador was very impressed. He wrote to King Louis: 'I swear, Sire, there is nothing finer to see than all this navy, nothing greater nor more majestic, than this great number of ships.'[9] Charles II gave him most lavish entertainment.

VII

Frustrated Negotiations

Ralph Montagu, Second son of Lord Montagu of Boughton, who later served as British ambassador in France, acquired his early experience in diplomacy charged by Charles II on special missions to France.

It is almost certain that Madame is referring to young Ralph Montagu then aged twenty-four and not to the Abbé Montagu (though her letter is endorsed 'Dutchesse of Orléans by L'Ab. Montegu') when she wrote to King Charles from Paris on 2 January 1663.

> I will not importune you with too long a letter, since Mr Montague is very well informed of everything here and has even had a very pleasant visit thanks to the good treatment he received from those in authority.[1]

She tells him that she has detained his special messenger Bruno: she explains in her charming, humorous way that she is to blame, 'I do not think your rage (colère) will be very great,' she added.

Ralph Montagu brought back to London enthusiastic accounts of the gaiety and magnificence of the French Court. Molière's comedy *L'Ecole des Femmes* was performed at the Louvre and dedicated to Madame during March 1663. On 8 January the exquisite *Ballet des Arts* was performed for the first time at the Palais-Royal. The words were written by Benserade and Baptiste, the music composed by Lulli. Madame took the principal part in choosing the costumes together with the Duc de St. Aignan, and arranged the production. King Louis himself appeared as the chief shepherd, while Madame dressed in

77

a flowery hat, and gaudy ribbons took the role of the chief shepherdess, attended by four maidens, Louise de la Vallière, her
later rival the arrogant beautiful brunette Mlle. de Tonnay-
Charente, then engaged to the Marquis de Montespan, Mademoiselle de St. Simon, and lastly Mademoiselle de Sévigné.
There, too, was Mademoiselle de Sévigné's celebrated and
proud mother. Madame was superb in another role as Pallas
Athene, wearing a helmet on her head and dressed in a classic
costume. Her four maids were Amazons. Many years later long
after Madame's death, Madame de Sévigné would nostalgically evoke the scene: '*Ah! Quelles bergères et quelles amazones!*' she
cries, and then her tribute to the Duchess of Orléans, '*Madame,
que les siècles entiers auront peine a remplacer, et pour la beauté et pour
la belle jeunesse et pour la danse.*' When Ralph Montagu returned
to Charles II's court, the King teased his sister that he
wondered Monsieur had allowed him to remain so long in
France, 'for he is undoubtedly in love with you'. He had given
King Charles II 'a very fine sword and belt, which I do not
believe was out of pure liberality, but because I am your
brother'.

It is evident that by October 1662 Madame had assumed
a position of importance as intermediary between her brother
and Louis XIV. He wrote to her on 26 October:

> And if it pleases you to propose to him that we may communi-
> cate our thoughts to each other in our own hands by this
> private channel I shall be very glad, knowing how much this
> mutual confidence will contribute towards maintaining our
> friendship.

Charles had not a great deal of confidence in Denzil, Lord
Holles, the new English Ambassador appointed to that position
during June 1663. He was a diligent, conscientious and honest
man, but he lacked finesse and subtlety in dealing with the
French. Charles told her:

> My Lord Holles writes such letters of you, as I am afraid

78

he is in love with you, and they say his wife begins already to be jealous of you.

Charles believed that Cominges whilst an ambassador in London did nothing to improve the relations between the two countries.

Tiresome disputes concerning precedence and etiquette were instrumental in worsening the relations between rival powers, in the seventeenth century. Louis XIV, for instance, insisted that his ambassadors should have precedence over the diplomatic representatives of all other princes and states and especially of Spain. However, a serious dispute had erupted over the precedence of the coaches of the last French Ambassador the Comte d'Estrades, and the Spanish Ambassador, the Baron de Watteville during 1661. So as to avoid further trouble when Monsieur de Cominges made his official entrée, King Charles now ordained that the coaches of foreign diplomatic representatives must be prevented from following the coaches of any new foreign ambassador on his entrée. On the instructions of King Louis, Cominges asked that the decree should be rescinded.[2]

As he was anxious 'not to leave any shadow of doubt in the mind of the King, my brother in regard to the perfect friendship established between us', Charles decided to send John Trevor as special envoy to explain the matter to Louis. Minette, too, used her diplomatic gifts to great advantage, smoothing the matter over. Trevor succeeded in effecting a compromise whereby it was agreed that only sovereign powers could make decrees concerning the conduct of ambassadors. Louis, however, was prepared to agree to the French Ambassador making his entrée without being followed by the coaches of other Foreign Diplomats. Cominges wrote to the French Foreign minister Lionne that there were no official incidents on his entrée, though he was unpopular. English ambassadors were likewise sensitive about their privileges and matters of etiquette. Their insistence was to cause much friction at the Court of France. Charles II thought that Lord Holles's arrival in Paris would increase the hopes of a close alliance between England and France, but he was quite incapable of establishing a confidential relationship with Louis XIV. He was of a cantankerous, stubborn disposition, more concerned with claiming his privileges as Charles's representative than in working for an alliance between the two countries. As for Monsieur de Cominges, King Charles II complained to Madame that 'he is not very foreward in the businesse'.[3] Cominges was always complaining of the English climate and did not much care for the English. Clarendon himself, obstinate and insular by nature, found Cominges difficult to negotiate with. It was unfortunate that the French Alliance was delayed for several years owing to the unsuitability of the two ambassadors representing the Kings of England and France. Charles turned more and more to his sister when relations between himself and Louis became a little strained.

When King Charles heard from his sister during May 1663 of King Louis's serious illness—he had caught measles from the Queen—he immediately sent Lord Mandeville, elder son of the Lord Chamberlain the Earl of Manchester to France, to inquire about King Louis's health. He made a rapid recovery. While his life had been in jeopardy, Madame with her customary courage had visited the King, absolutely regardless of the risks she was incurring.

During 1663, Charles's letters to Minette are about serious political matters and his intimate private concerns. She was extremely agitated when she learnt that George Digby Second Earl of Bristol had made an attack on Lord Clarendon in the House of Lords, accusing him of High Treason. Cominges, who never managed to understand the English, professed himself astonished that Bristol was allowed to walk about as usual and enjoy the diversion of playing bowls, instead of being assigned to the Bastille. It was surprising that he should be permitted to accuse Lord Clarendon of such serious offences, especially as Clarendon was the father-in-law of the Duke of York. Surely England was heading for another Commonwealth.

Charles was an indolent, but very entertaining letter writer.

He writes to his sister on 20 April 1663 to tell her about his son the Duke of Monmouth's marriage to the Lady Anna Scott, Countess of Buccleuch. They were both children. 'I am goeing to sup with them,' wrote Charles, 'where we intend to dance and see them to bed together, but the ceremony shall stop there, for they are both to young to lye all nighte together ...'

Queen Catherine of Braganza was very anxious to obtain a little book of devotions in Spanish. 'Pray send two of them,' Charles requested his sister. James Hamilton, groom of the Bedchamber to Charles II was a frequent visitor to France, and was entrusted with messages and letters for Minette. 'I have nothing so neere my harte, as how I may finde occasions to expresse that tender passion I have for my dearest Minette.' Their contemporaries in England, influenced by a hatred of Roman Catholicism, spread a malicious rumour, that there was an incestuous relationship between brother and sister, but this is too absurd to consider in any serious light.

He constantly sends her quaint little inquiries:

I desire to know whether it be the fasion in France for the women to make use of such a large size of wax as the peece you sent me [wax for sealing letters], our women heere finde the size a little extravagant, yet I beleeve when they shall know that 'tis the fasion there, they will be willing enough to submit to it.

When Catherine of Braganza fell seriously ill, during the winter of 1663, King Louis sent over one of his gentlemen in Ordinary, M. de Catheux. The French ambassador, M. de Cominges informed Lionne, his Foreign Minister, that Catheux was admitted into the Queen's bedchamber. According to Cominges, 'Her illness has made her so deaf, that she could not hear at all unless you shouted in her ear.'[4] Charles, who was now very fond of his Portuguese-born wife, thanked his sister and Monsieur 'for the great part you take in the recovery of my wife'. 'She mends very slowly,' he wrote, 'and continues still so weak as she cannot yett stande upon her leggs.'

On one occasion Charles sent a messenger named Slaughter with a present to his brother-in-law Monsieur, of four good horses. They were very hard to find in England, particularly during the years 1666 and 1667.

For almost three vital years from July 1663, My lord Holles served as English Ambassador in Paris. Bishop Gilbert Burnet his contemporary wrote a shrewd character sketch of this man.[5] 'He had the soul of an old stubborn Roman in him,' and obstinacy was indeed his outstanding quality. Burnet continued:

> He was a faithful but a rough friend, and a severe but fair enemy. He had a true sense of religion, and was a man of an unblameable course of life, and of a sound judgement when it was not biassed by passion.

One need not take seriously the French Ambassador Barillon's later accusation that Holles accepted bribes from Louis XIV. Although by temperament a Puritan, Denzil Holles had opposed Oliver Cromwell, and both men had detested each other. For this 'the old stubborn Roman' must have earned the approval of Charles II. He was created a peer for his part in bringing about the Restoration. His interesting correspondence among the State Papers of France in the Public Record Office show his growing hostility to the Commercial, political aspirations and projects of Louis XIV.

The trouble with Holles was that he was more occupied in fiercely contesting points of etiquette and privilege than in working steadily for an alliance with France. Both Madame and her brother were to be very much irritated by Holles's insistence on trifles. Nevertheless Holles soon succumbed to Madame's charm.

The new ambassador was well aware of the disputes about the precedence of ambassadorial coaches at Cominges' entrée, and when the Princes of the Blood at the French Court claimed that their coaches should take precedence over his during his reception by King Louis, he fiercely resisted their arguments. His temper was not improved owing to the gout that afflicted him when first arriving on French soil. Although Charles was impatient with his ambassador for insisting too much on trifles, he decided to support Holles in standing out for his rights. Indeed as Charles wrote his sister there were precedents in the cases of Sir Thomas Edmonds, my Lord Scudamore and the Earl of Leicester, all of whom had been ambassadors in France. Charles II would have really preferred that the ceremonial entrée did not take place.

Meanwhile Cominges had taken umbrage when invited to a dinner by the Lord Mayor of London during the autumn of 1663. When he arrived at this function, he was enraged to find that his fellow guests, the Lord Chancellor Clarendon and most of the Council already seated. Nobody had the courtesy to get up to receive him, although Cominges arrived a little late. The Ambassador left immediately for his house, and lost no time in complaining to King Louis of the slight. He described it as *'incivilité grossière et barbare'*.[6] Louis did not take the matter too seriously and was concerned lest the King of England should be troubled with it. He told Madame not to mention the incident to her brother, but she had already been too precipitate in doing so. She asked Lord Holles to write to King Charles requesting him not to take any notice of the information she had given him.[7] When he attended the Lord Mayor's Banquet a year later, the Lord Mayor and Aldermen took great care to offer him every civility.

By her tact, Madame helped the King of France to reach a satisfactory decision in the tiresome dispute concerning Lord Holles's official entrée. It was decided that it should be abandoned. Instead, the ambassador was received by King Louis in an audience at St. Germain, but the Princes of the Blood were not present on this occasion.

Lord Holles corresponded frequently with Sir Henry Bennet, later Lord Arlington, Charles II's principal secretary of state.

Some of the letters were in cypher, and the Ambassador complains during February 1664:

> The cypher it seemes was done in hast by him that writt for you, for he mistooke very much. A little mistake in the writer may cause a great one in ye actor.

He also expressed his fear that his letters were being tampered with. In those days few diplomats or politicians cared to entrust important communications to the 'ordinary', the official post which delivered letters once a week in Paris and London. When storms raged in the Channel, posts were often delayed owing to the packet-boats being held up in the ports. That is why the King and Madame preferred their highly confidential correspondence to be carried by some trusted confidant or servant. However, on one occasion a letter of Charles's to his sister written in December 1663 arrived in a sodden state because the packet-boat had been wrecked in a storm.[8] There is no trace of this letter.

Holles could never be certain that his confidential reports to Sir Henry Bennet, who had been an intimate friend of King Charles during his exile, were not opened. It is a pleasure to read the letters of the elderly, irascible Holles, for his handwriting is beautifully clear. On one occasion with an air of triumph he wrote to Harry Bennet on 22 May 1664: 'I have received yours of May 16st, I am confident a virgin unviolated by the way, which it seemes is not the portion of all that passe.' Holles made various experiments in devising means of preventing his letters being opened. He considered that strong glue as well as wax seals were instrumental in combating this menace. Cominges, who certainly had a poor opinion of Englishmen, wrote with slight irony to King Louis: 'They possess here the secret of opening letters more subtly than anywhere else in the world.'

Holles evidently formed a high opinion of Madame, and pays tribute to her dexterity and wisdom in his letters.

During February 1664 Madame was again enceinte, and it

was unfortunate that whilst taking part in a masque at the Louvre that she stumbled and fell and might have knocked her head against a silver grate had she not been caught by a French gentleman M. de Clérembault. Although not seriously hurt, she had sprained her ankle and was obliged to rest for a few days.

Charles on hearing of Minette's accident immediately wrote her to express his great relief that she had sustained no harm. There is a humorous touch in his letter (29 February) very typical of him:

> We have the same disease of sermons that you complaine of there, but I hope you have the same convenience that the rest of the family has, of sleeping out most of the time, which is a great ease to those who are bounde to hear them.... I praye send me some wax to seale letters that has gold in it, for there is none to be gott in this towne.

On 19 May he writes from Whitehall:

> I have been all this afternoone playing the good husband haveing been abroade with my wife and 'tis now past twelve a clock and I am very sleepy.

He alludes to a quarrel that had broken out at The Hague between William Prince of Orange and the Comte D'Estrades, now French ambassador in Holland. The Comte had refused to give way in his coach to the Prince. There is no mention of the matter in any of Madame's surviving letters to her brother, but no doubt she would have considered D'Estrades's complaint somewhat trivial.

During the summer of 1664 Madame was becoming increasingly exasperated with Lord Holles for his insistence on trifling matters. She wrote to Charles from Fontainebleau on 22 June (22 May is erased).

> It is perfectly right that he [Lord Holles] should have privileges, but when it is not the custom of the country and the King [Louis] offers to deprive Cominges of them, there can to my mind be no answer. My Lord Hollis is offended with

Lionne [French Foreign Minister] because he will not give him the style of 'Excellency'. He had always done so, but my lord Hollis never styled him so in return, so that he got tired of it.... I am in despair [she admitted] for I think that it is very disappointing [facheux] that everything should be held up for things of this kind. I am called for to go to the Comedy, which is why I have only the time to assure you that I am your very humble servant.[9]

It is a matter for regret that Minette's letter to her brother in which she describes her little girl Marie-Louise now a lovely child of two years old is missing: she told Charles that Marie-Louise was exactly like him. She also wrote that she had invested some money on behalf of Mademoiselle (as she was called) in the newly formed French East India Company.[10] In his reply Charles wrote her: 'I see you are as hot upon setting up an East India Company at Paris, as we are here upon our Guinea trade.' He refers to the commercial rivalry between Britain and the Dutch, and the necessity to send a strong convoy of a man-of-war to protect the fleet in case the Dutch were to attack it, 'in revenge for our taking the fort of Cape Verde'. He was flattered that his sister should think that his niece closely resembled him 'for I never thought my face was even so much as intended for a beauty. I wish with all my heart I could see her, for at this distance I love her....'

Lord Holles refers to the forthcoming birth of Madame's infant son Philippe-Charles in a letter written on 25 June to Sir Henry Bennet in which he tactfully alludes to the Secretary of State recovery in health from an illness:

Seeing it is His Majesty's pleasure that I go to visit the Princess, it shall be done onely I must stay till I can speake with my Lord Abbot Montague, who went Munday last to Fountainebleau and I doubt will returne till Madame be brought to bed....

On 16 July Madame gave birth to an infant son—somewhat belatedly. Philippe-Charles first saw the light between nine and

ten o'clock on a Wednesday morning. There was great rejoicing, throughout France, especially as the Dauphin was known
to be sickly. Monsieur could hardly restrain his delight and
wrote the same day to his brother-in-law Charles II to give him
the glad news.

> I should fail of the duty which I owe your Majesty [he told
> him] if I did not hasten to inform you that your Sister was
> this morning safely delivered of a fine boy. The child seems
> to be in excellent health, and will, I hope grow up worthy
> of your Majesty's friendship, which I ask you to bestow upon
> him. . . . I send Boyer, my first maitre d'hotel with this.

Philippe-Charles was a lusty baby, and Madame asked her
beloved brother to be his god-father (*parrain*). She loved her
only son more than Marie-Louise. Madame de Mottville relates
in her *Memoires* that he was created Duc de Valois, so as to
revive (*ressusciter*) in him this famous line that has given such
great kings to France. Is it possible that Madame de La Fayette,
who loved to create Valois history, suggested this title to her
friend? Madame's private life was unhappy at this period.
Her relations with Monsieur had further deteriorated, for he
showed her quite clearly that he preferred the companionship
of his male minions to her own society. Occasionally she heard
news of the Comte de Guiche, who was now fighting against
the Russians in Poland. He had distinguished himself by his
valour, and had been gravely wounded during one battle. A
bullet had struck his chest and had completely destroyed a case
containing Madame's portrait, which he carried near his heart.
The Princess had sworn to King Louis that she would never
see her admirer again, and had demanded the return of some
letters she had written to him in Lorraine. That she still entertained very tender sentiments for this chivalrous nobleman is
certain.

In de Guiche's absence many young courtiers had lost their
hearts to Madame. The Prince de Marsillac, eldest son of the
Duc de La Rochefoucauld, fell so ardently in love that he

aroused Monsieur's jealousy. Consequently the young man's
father was obliged to send him away from Court. It was not
as if the Duchess of Orléans encouraged the attentions of Monsieur d'Armagnac, Grand Ecuyer de France. She found them
embarrassing. She asked the Archbishop of Sens to intervene,
and d'Armagnac no longer pestered her.

Far the most dangerous of the Princess's would-be lovers was
the unscrupulous Marquis de Vardes, well versed in the art of
paying Court to ladies of high birth. Everybody at Court knew
that he enjoyed the favours of Olympia Comtesse de Soissons
and that Madame d'Armagnac had also been his mistress.
There is no doubt that Madame behaved extremely indiscreetly
in her relations with de Vardes. It was folly on her part to show
him some of her brother's letters, so that the man acquired a
hold over her. One can only suppose that she knew that King
Louis rather liked de Vardes and sometimes confided in him.
According to Madame de La Fayette, the Comte du Plessis,
First gentleman of the Bedchamber to Monsieur, '*par un complai-
sance extraordinaire*' for Madame, was the bearer of the letters
she wrote to him and of those that de Vardes sent in return.
Vardes was not the sort of man who would be content for long
with a platonic relationship with any woman. Ultimately he
wanted their bodies, and Madame had in her nature some elu-
sive quality, something divine that attracted the devil in
Vardes. She may at first have found the tall man with his
leonine head attractive, but she only wanted his friendship. In
any case she was aware that the Comtesse de Soissons was his
mistress. However, he was intelligent enough to get into
Madame's good graces.

One day when a group of courtiers, including de Vardes,
surrounded Madame, a messenger arrived with news that the
Comte de Guiche had been seriously wounded in Poland.
According to Madame de La Fayette, Madame said, her sym-
pathetic nature moved to pity by the dangers that the Comte
had encountered, 'I believe I care more for the Comte de
Guiche than I knew before.' A heavy scowl appeared on de

Vardes's face, and from this time he determined, if possible, to ruin Madame and de Guiche, although formerly his friend. Baffled in his desire to make Madame his mistress and wounded in his self-esteem, he hastened to King Louis to pour into his ears that Madame, his sister-in-law was engaged in a treacherous correspondence with her brother. Indeed, he alleged that the King of France had been mentioned in a disparaging way in these letters. De Vardes mischievously used every artifice to destroy his master's confidence in her. For some time Louis's sentiments towards the Princess of England were clouded by suspicion. All the same King Louis was on the whole very kind to Madame during the summer.

Madame wrote a long letter to the Queen Catherine her sister-in-law complaining of de Varde's behaviour. Her brother refers to it when he tells her:

> I did not thinke it possible that some persons could have had so ill a part in that matter, as I see they have had by your letter. I shall have by this a better opinion of my devotion for the time to come, for I am of those bigotts, who thinke that malice is a much greater sinn than a poore, frailety of nature.

While they were still on friendly terms, de Vardes had done his utmost to blacken the reputation of the Comte de Guiche. Pretending still to be his friend, he wrote witty letters to de Guiche, while he was overseas, alluding to Madame's alleged infidelities, her affairs with other men. They had the effect of making the unhappy man jealous and suspicius. He was stung almost to madness.

During the summer (1664) Olympia Countess de Soissons was extremely ill and had at last revealed de Vardes's baseness to Madame. De Vardes asked for an interview with Madame and bursting into tears in a most contrite way begged her forgiveness. If only she would become his ally, he would conceal her dealings with de Guiche. Madame scornfully rejected his offer. She was now aware that de Vardes had shown one of de Guiche's letters to King Louis, a proof that Princess Henriette was breaking her promise to have no further communications with de Guiche.

When he returned to France from Poland, the Comte de Guiche received the King's permission to appear at Court so long as he did not actually enter Madame's presence. He had learnt of de Vardes's treachery, and in a towering rage challenged his former friend either to confess his guilt or to fight. In vain he desperately tried to obtain interviews with Madame, but she refused to see him. He asked the beautiful English-born Elizabeth Hamilton Comtesse de Gramont, who was then in Paris and on most cordial terms with Madame, to intercede for him. Charles had described her in a letter to Minette: 'She is as good a creature as ever lived.' In his characteristic way he adds: 'I beleeve she will passe for a handsome woman in France, though she has not yett, since her lying in, recovered that good shape she had before, and I am affraide never will.' Madame only relented so far as to let de Guiche know that she realized that he was innocent of the false accusations brought against him and that she recognised him as a man of honour.

It was a relief to Madame to accompany the King and Queen to Vincennes on 13 August, for Monsieur remained at the Palais-Royal in Paris with their two children. Lord Holles visited Madame in Vincennes and reported home:

> She looks as well as ever I saw her look in my life, that is as well as possible; and is grown so fat, that my compliment to her yesterday was, it was well she had good witnesses, else nobody would believe she had brought forth such a lusty young duke, to see her in so good a plight so soon, and the young duke is as lusty and fine a child as ever I saw.

During the early autumn she went with Monsieur to his country house of Villers-Cotterets, a royal Chateau built by François I, surrounded by forests near the town of Laon. Madame may have felt the strain of the last few months when she was deeply troubled by the intrigues of her enemies, the

90

Comte de Vardes and the Comtesse de Soissons. She felt ill and depressed. Guy Patin wrote of her: 'She is slender, and delicate, and of the number of those whom Hippocrates says have an inclination towards phthisis.'[11] It was a kind of consumption and Patin considered that English people were particularly likely to catch it. Her doctor prescribed for her a simple diet of asses milk, and her health was so much improved that she and Monsieur were able to entertain King Louis, the Queen Marie-Thérèse and the Prince de Condé to a grand fête at Villers-Cotterets where a performance of Molière's *Tartuffe* was given before the royal visitors.

During October Madame moved to Versailles, and one of her letters in the Lambeth Palace Library to her brother alludes to the progress of the fine new Palace King Louis was building around the original hunting-lodge erected by his father Louis XIII. It seems strange but almost all of the French King's contemporaries complained of Louis's extravagance, particularly his thrifty minister Jean Baptiste Colbert. The genius of the landscape gardener Le Nôtre, the architect Le Vau, Mansart and others were to make Versailles a magnificent palace. Minette told her brother:

> The King is making a great building here which will be a great ornament to this place and which adjoins the forecourt in the form of a triangle. The convenience of this is that it will cost him nothing, for he is giving space to a number of persons of quality who will build at their own expense and are very glad to have houses of which the site had been given them.[12]

In the same letter she mentions that she has discovered six months ago various jewels and valuables. These had formerly belonged 'to the King our father'. She informed her brother that she had put in prison those responsible for the theft. Among the valuables were a very beautiful diamond hat-band, also a garter, a good many rings and a portrait of Prince Henry (Duke of Gloucester) surrounded with very big diamonds. Minette suggested that Charles should ask the Queen (Henrietta Maria) whether she recognized them as Charles I's property, 'for the King possessed nothing she did not know about'. Lord Holles also informed Madame that he was making independent inquiries. Knowing how touchy the British ambassador was, Madame wanted him to take the matter over. According to documents in the Public Record Office[13] the articles also included a magnificent diamond, a crystal ship set with pearls and rubies, a George and some pieces of tapestry. None of the valuables were ever recovered.

On 12 November she wrote from Paris telling him of Queen Marie-Thérèse's serious illness. She had terrible pains in the legs 'and the attacks of tertian are still marked'. The bearer of Madame's letter was Mr. Sidney, (possibly Henry Sidney, later Earl of Romney). As Marie-Thérèse was pregnant and shortly expecting a child, the King was very anxious and sat up the whole of one night by the Queen's bedside. The Queen's illness had serious repercussions, for it caused her to fall, prematurely, into labour. The Queen-Mother Anne of Austria was vexed to see her daughter-in-law Madame looking extremely elegant at the Queen's bedside with her hair arranged in yellow ribands. Marie-Thérèse's daughter only lived for a month. Holles's report to Sir Henry Bennet is very curious:

> There is a strange report of ye little Madame, wch I should not write if it were not commonly spoken, that she hath the colour and visage of a blackamore, caused it seemes by the Queenes usually seeing some young Negroes wch hath been sent to ye K^d from Gigeri, and so working upon her imagination, wch hath sometimes wrought such effects upon women with child.[14]

Cominges from London was very sceptical of the truth of this allegation. He took every opportunity to ridicule Holles saying that his French was so poor that he had misunderstood his informant to say 'une fille maure', instead of 'une fille morte'. However, there were rumours about this alleged Moorish infant in

France, and Madame de Montpensier who actually saw the baby, wrote that her strange appearance was owing to the Queen seeing these young negroes. Poor Queen, so jealous and so naïve! Madame de Motteville relates that on one occasion after her return from Normandy she visited the Queen. From a window she could see Mademoiselle de La Vallière, who was on her way to sup with the Comtesse de Soissons. She said to her in Spanish: '*Esta donzella con las anacadas de diamante, es esta que el Rei quiere*':* Madame de Motteville found it a hard task to explain to Marie-Thérèse that all husbands without ceasing to love their wives are often unfaithful in that manner. That certainly applied to Kings and courtiers of the late seventeenth century both in France and England.

* This girl who has the pendants of diamonds is the one who the King loves.

VIII

The Second Dutch War

Throughout 1664, Charles II was growing increasingly apprehensive that he would be unable to avoid a war with the Dutch. His correspondence with his beloved sister reflects his anxiety. He was extremely uncertain about Louis XIV's attitude if war should break out, since he was well aware that France by the Treaty of 1662 had pledged her assistance to Holland. There was the growing commercial rivalry between the two nations in the East Indies and on the West Coast of Africa, and the question of maritime supremacy had not been settled by the first Anglo-Dutch war (1652–4).[1] On 2 June he had mentioned to his sister that Sir George Downing, then ambassador at The Hague, had just arrived in England from Holland.

> I never saw [wrote Charles] so greate an appetite to a warre as in both this towne and country, espetially in the Parliament Men who I am confident would pawne their estates to maintaine a war, but all this shall not governe me, for I will looke meerly what is wise and best for the honour and good of England and will be very steady in what I resolve, and if I be forced to a warre, I shall be ready with as good ships and men as ever was seene, and leave the successe to God.[2]

It is evident that both Charles II and Madame ardently desired an English alliance with France, and Madame was inclined to blame England for retarding it. Charles thought that the fault lay with the ambassadors. He wrote on 23 August:

> if the ambassadors on both sides have had the misfortune to render themselves unacceptable where they negotiate why

94

must it be thought there master's fault? ... you shall see now that my Lord Hollis will goe on very roundly in the matter so as there shall be no neglect on our part. ...

Charles feared that Louis's friendly overtures to the Dutch would hinder the proposed alliance with France. The situation was now so delicate that he had far more faith in his sister's tactful intervention with Louis than in his own ambassador.

In a letter written from Whitehall on 24 October, Charles wrote:

> You will have heard of our takeing of New Amsterdam which lies just by New England. Tis a place of great importance to trade, and a very goode town, it did belong to England heertofore, but the Dutch by degrees drove our people out of it, and built a very good towne but we have gott the better of it, and tis now called New Yorke. He that tooke it and is now there, is Nichols my brother's [James Duke of York] servant who you know very well.[3]

It is fascinating to read this letter of Charles in the Quai D'Orsay collection with its casual allusion to what was in fact a very important matter. Governor Richard Nicolls of Massachusetts* had succeeded in capturing New Amsterdam. The repercussions were of enormous significance. The Dutch lost their foothold in North America, and the capture of New Amsterdam led to the linking up of the New England provinces with the English settlement of Virginia.

Madame's importance as a link between Charles and Louis was emphasized during the autumn (1664). She wrote from Paris to her brother on 4 November:

> I have shown your last letter to the King [Louis XIV] who commanded me to tell you in reply to what you wrote to me concerning the Dutch that if you are willing to treat his subjects in England like the English he will consent to do

---

* First governor of New York.

the same for the English in France except for the 50 sols. I am not clever [habille] enough to understand what this means, but they are the very words which the King told me to repeat to you, and I am doing so.[4]

There was a tax of fifty sols per ton taken from all foreign ships entering French ports. Fouquet was responsible for this measure, and Colbert had adhered to it.

At this juncture both Charles and Louis both sent envoys on semi-official missions to France. Charles chose his intimate friend Charles Berkeley, Lord Fitzharding. According to Cominges he had more influence with the King of England than anybody else at this period. Clarendon disliked him, but he may have been consumed by jealousy, for Fitzharding was a rising man. Many people however, liked him for he was loyal, generous and good-natured. Fitzharding's mission was successful, for he saw both King Louis and Madame, who mentions him in her letters. Even Holles had to admit that Fitzharding's tact had made his work easier.

The King of France's envoy the Marquis de Ruvigny was well chosen, since, unlike Cominges, he was much respected and trusted by Charles II. He was a Protestant nobleman with influential English connections, for his sister had married the Earl of Southampton. Not only did he understand the English character, but he had a good knowledge of English.

Minette wrote an important letter to Charles from Paris on 28 November and as Ruvigni was about to leave for England asked him to deliver it to her brother. Ruvigni's real work was to report to King Louis the state of English feeling towards France. It might be thought that Cominges would resent Ruvigni's mission, but they were in fact intimate friends and he even welcomed it.

I could not let Ruvigni leave [wrote Madame] without giving him this letter to show you that you will see by what he tells me how much your friendship is desired and even necessary here. In God's name take advantage of this and do not lose any time in obtaining the King's secret promise that he will not help the Dutch for you understand he cannot promise you this openly because of his engagements with them, though it is notorious that they are only worth what one makes them worth as the saying is. But as in this world appearances must be kept up and this affair requires them, you ought as I have already said to content yourself with a secret agreement, which in this way will be much more solid and I promise you to see to it that it is done in good faith ...[5]

Like her brother, she thought Ruvigni 'a very honest man'. Madame's contemporaries bear witness that her own nature was very straightforward.

At this period when Madame was deeply anxious about the political situation she reached a crisis in her own personal affairs. Vardes, who had aspired to make Madame his mistress, was now her bitter enemy. One day towards the end of 1664, a group of courtiers were gathered in the Queen's apartments teasing the young, handsome Chevalier de Lorraine, who was having an affair with Mlle. de Fiennes, one of Madame's maids-of-honour.

The Chevalier de Lorraine was a favourite of Monsieur's, though he only discovered Lorraine's pursuit of Mlle. de Fiennes much later, and was then devoured by jealousy. Among the courtiers in the Queen's apartments was the sinister Marquis de Vardes, who said in a sneering voice to Lorraine: 'I do not understand why you bother about the maid when you could easily have the mistress.' The insult was repeated to Madame by the Maréchal de Gramont. Stung by de Vardes's insolence, and his offence seemed all the greater since her intense pride was hurt as a Princess of England, she immediately complained to King Louis. She implored him to dismiss Vardes from Court. Louis was loath to take this course, but agreed to it. Meanwhile Vardes, who had learnt in advance what the King intended, had of his own accord gone to the Bastille and requested the governor to imprison him. The governor at once went to King Louis to ascertain his pleasure, and he told him to keep Vardes a prisoner. His friends now very foolishly made a great clamour at Court, for they asserted publicly that the King in reality had been most unwilling to punish Vardes. Deeply troubled, Madame again went to the King, and told him that for the sake of her own honour and that of the royal family Vardes must be banished.

Madame evidently took it very much to heart, and one must remember that she had endured much from this wretched man in the past and could no longer brook his insolence. She wrote from Paris to her brother on 17 December:

> As I have already told you, it is an affair that will have terrible consequences if they are not avoided by exiling this man, since all France is interested in it, and if I have to bear the consequences since it is on my account judge of what might happen! I hope that your intervention will settle everything and will extricate me from this business.

She told Charles that if the matter was not settled as she wanted 'it will be a scandal that any private citizen should have been able to defy me and have the King's (Louis's) support'.[6] As it transpired, Charles's intervention was not necessary, for King Louis ordered Vardes to leave the Bastille and to retire to his own government of Aigues-Mortes. When he eventually returned to Court many years later, he wore the same dress, now absurdly out of fashion, in which he had been banished. 'When one displeases your Majesty,' he wittily remarked, 'one is not only wretched but ridiculous.'

As if freed of a great burden, Minette's letters to Charles now become lighter in tone. During the winter of 1664/5 a comet or what Chares had referred to as 'a blazing starr' had appeared in the sky, and excited much speculation both in England and France. Supersitious people—and Charles was not among them—thought that it boded no good, while the optimists regarded it as a favourable omen. It was followed by another comet a few days later. Charles, who, as is well known, was keenly interested in science and astronomy, wrote to his sister: 'Pray inquire of the skillfull men and let me know whether it has been seen in Paris.' Her reply is an example of her marked sense of humour and her endearing sense of fun.

> I will tell you [she wrote] that there have been meetings at the Jesuits' Observatory which were attended by all the learned persons and also by those who are not. The former disputed according to their belief which were nearly all at variance, some say it is the same comet returned and others that it is a new one. And as one would have to get there to discover the truth I suppose it will remain undecided.... This is all that my ignorance permits me to tell you and I think that it is enough to satisfy your curiosity. Since these learned gentlemen are beyond question all mad [tout fous] or very nearly so.[7]

It seems probable that Minette inherited her sense of humour from her maternal grandfather Henri Quatre.

Her reference, too, to Madame de Cominges on 20 February (1665), who had just returned to Paris after a most fatiguing journey, 'looking so well and so fat (grose) that were that the only reason for making me long to go to England I would do so with all my heart', is not without a touch of malice. The former Sybille d'Amalbi was much admired for her wit and beauty, and her tendency to have affairs outside matrimony may have given her husband some anxiety.

It so happened about this time that Monsieur and Madame were invited to a masked ball by Madame de La Vieuville. They arrived in a hired coach, so as to conceal their identity. As they entered the hall, Monsieur suggested that they should join up with another masked party. Monsieur, who was in a good humour, gave his hand to one of the masked ladies, and Madame took the hand of an unknown gentleman.

'Judge of her surprise when she found that it was the crippled hand of M. De Guiche, who at the same moment recognized

"Madame" by the perfume which she used for her hair.'[8] De Guiche's three fingers had been maimed during the wars. For the romantic de Guiche it was heavenly to be mounting the staircase with the woman he had loved in vain for so long and to recognize her perfume of carnation. They could hardly restrain from crying out. There were hurried explanations; the need for speed was urgent, since Monsieur was approaching. As she turned to join her husband, she slipped and would have fallen down a flight of stairs had not the gallant Comte caught her in his arms. What a strange chance had brought Madame and de Guiche together again!

She had given her word that she would not see him again and she was faithful to it. It is said that desperate to obtain a final interview with Madame, de Guiche disguised himself as a valet in the livery of La Vallière, the royal mistress, and stood in the Courtyard of the Palais-Royal to see Madame pass by on her way to the Louvre. He tried to speak to her, but his strength failed him and he fainted. They were never to meet again. De Guiche soon left for Holland where he later served with distinction in a naval battle against England.

Madame was not yet twenty-one and the affair with de Guiche had given her far more pain than pleasure. She was now a sadder and wiser woman. As for de Guiche, his love of Madame undoubtedly brought him deep sorrow, but as Madame de Motteville observed his vanity deprived them of much of their bitterness. Madame de La Fayette considered that Madame's feeling for him was never very deep.

Certainly after the exile of the Marquis de Vardes, her relations with her mother-in-law Anne of Austria were much improved. There was a growing tendency to become more serious.

One bitter enemy with whom Madame had once been on friendly terms could not forgive her for being instrumental in exiling de Vardes; this was the Comtesse de Soissons, who now informed King Louis that the Comte de Guiche had written letters to 'Madame' in which the King was very disrespectfully treated. She also informed King Louis that the Comte had advised Madame to take possession of Dunkirk, handed over by the English to the French some time before, in her brother's name, and that he had offered her a regiment of guards for this purpose. It may well be that Madame was opposed to the sale of Dunkirk, but she managed to persuade King Louis that there was no truth in Olympia's allegations against de Guiche. The Comtesse de Soissons was banished to Champagne and Vardes was moved from Aigues-Mortes to the citadel of Mont-pelier where he remained a prisoner for two years.

Relations between the English and the Dutch had deteriorated during the winter (1664). The able Dutch ambassador in Paris van Beuninghen, who had signed the original treaty with the French in 1662, was doing his utmost to obtain the promise of French support in the event of an Anglo-Dutch war, which seemed inevitable. Charles was well aware that van Beuninghen was making trouble with the French, trying to brand him as the aggressor. Minette's invaluable role as his intermediary 'with the K. my brother' (Louis) had become all the more vital. He wrote his sister on 12 January:

> I will lett him know what my pretensions are, that van Beun-
> inghen may not have the least pretence to say that I desire
> warre for warre sake, for I know that he does use all sortes
> of artes to make me the agressore, and does not stick to affirme
> matters of fact which are not true, and which will be proved
> to be so.

In one letter in the Quai D'Orsay archives,[9] Charles told his sister: 'My inclinations are to give my friendship to France, but if that cannot be had I am not so inconsiderable but that I can make very considerable friendships elsewhere. . . .' He preferred the friendship with France, particularly because Minette was there. In almost all his letters he complains of the unhelpful attitude of Cominges, and he had far more faith in Ruvigni's sincerity.

Louis adopted a policy of complete self-interest and Charles's motives were much the same. Louis was well aware that his father-in-law Philip IV of Spain was dangerously ill. If he died—and he expected this to occur quite shortly—he wanted to make a claim to the Spanish Netherlands in the name of his wife. What he really wished to accomplish was to build more ships, thus making his navy more powerful, so as to expand his maritime commerce.[10] So it suited him if the English and the Dutch were to exhaust their resources in their naval warfare, but he was watching the situation very closely, fearing lest either of the combatants should conquer the other and thus obtain undisputed dominion of the seas.

His personal feelings towards the Dutch were almost the same as 'his brother of England', for he disliked them intensely. He did not want to intervene in their favour, unless absolutely necessary. It was in his interests that an open declaration of war should be avoided, if possible.

For the purpose of trying to influence Charles to keep the status quo Louis decided to send two ambassadors to London to give assistance to Cominges. Henri de Bourbon, Duc de Verneuil, was related to both the kings of France and England for he was a son of Henri IV by his mistress Henriette de Balzac d'Entragues, Henri's last important concubine. He was likely to be congenial to Charles II, for he was a keen sportsman and had an expert knowledge of horses and hounds. His duties were really honorary. He was more in his element as Sir Keith Feiling observed,[11] at Newmarket than in the council chamber. Honoré de Courtin the second diplomat, a professional with an intimate knowledge of law, extremely cunning and astute, would be likely to appeal to Charles II, for he has been described 'as a jovial sinner who could understand Charles's ruling passion'.

In her letter of 20 February 1665 Madame alludes to the ambassadors' impending departure for London.

Relations between the United Provinces (Holland) and Britain were aggravated by an incident related by Madame to her brother on 3 March: 'The King has ordered me to tell you', she wrote, 'of a thing which has happened at Bordeaux, and

1 Henriette Anne d'Orléans in childhood, by Claude Mellan

2 Henriette Anne d'Orléans, from a portrait after P. Mignard
painted in about 1665

3 Philippe Duc d'Orléans, by P. Mignard

4 Louis XIV à Cheval, by Houasse

5 Duchesse de la Vallière, by J. Nocret

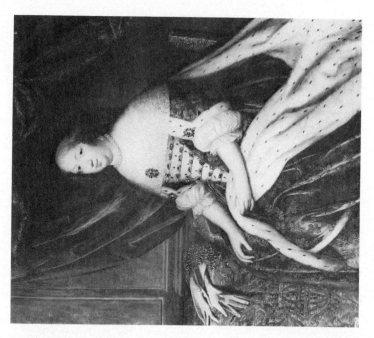

8 La Reine Anne d'Autriche, by J. Nocret

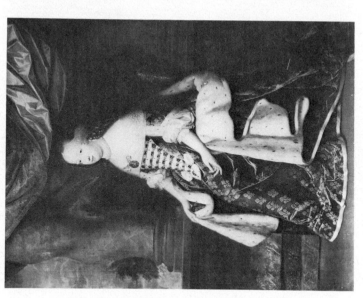

7 La Reine Marie-Thérèse, Ecole de P. Mignard

9 Charles II, after John Michael Wright

10 Henriette d'Angleterre, by A. Mathieu

11 Jean-Baptiste Molière, after A. C. Oypel

12 Jean Racine. Ecole de P. Mignard

13 Le Vicomte de Turenne. Ecole Français, seventeenth century

14 1st Lord Clifford of Chudleigh (Sir Thomas Clifford) by
Sir Peter Lely

15 La Duchesse d'Orléans, after Samuel Cooper

for which Milord Holles has asked justice.'[12] A Dutchman named Oyens whilst walking with an Englishman and other persons along the promenade made insulting remarks about Charles II and the Duke of York. Milord Holles had taken exception to these affronts as they concerned King Charles's honour. 'As a rule one does not pay much attention to what people say in the streets', wrote Madame. King Louis had told her that if her brother wished these men to be searched and punished, he would order it. In the same letter she informed him that the Duc de Verneuil was slightly ill, but she did not think that would delay his journey.

It is evident that Charles considered that Lord Holles had been a little officious in complaining about a point of honour. His reply to his sister is very characteristic of him, revealing his strong dislike of the Dutch.

> You know the old saying in England, the more a T. is stirred the more it stinkes, and so I think you have enough upon this clenly subject, which nothing but a stinking Duch man could have been the cause of … but pray thanke the King my brother and desire him not to take any kinde of notice of it, for such idle notices are not worth his anger or myne.

Lord Holles was very upset about it, resenting the imputation that he had been officious. He had been told of the incident by 'one Thompson an English merchant', he wrote Sir Henry Bennet. 'There were nine witnesses and substantial persons, who heard that Oyens the Dutch Man call the Duke of York Captaine of the Robbers.'[13]

A week later Madame wrote to Charles that she had heard stories of the cruelty of the Dutch in Guinea, 'appalling if it be true', she told him. She had also heard rumours that Englishmen had taken some Frenchmen prisoners making them suffer terrible tortures. She implored her brother to let her know the truth. 'Having such a generous soul,' she assured him, 'you would not suffer such things to be done to your enemies and far less to the French who are your friends.'[14]

Charles soon discovered that a 'duch man' pretending to be a Swedish seaman had given false evidence. 'He has been whipped through Cheapside,' he informed his sister. Unfortunately there was some truth in the allegations that French seamen had been badly treated by the English.

Perhaps Madame's most important letter in the Lambeth Palace series is the one proposing a secret alliance with King Louis, and she could hardly have proposed this without Louis's knowledge. She wrote Charles from Paris, referring openly to Louis's designs on the Netherlands. In exchange for the secret treaty it was suggested that Charles might promise Louis his support for his Flanders plans, 'seeing that the King of Spain* is in bad health, and which will surely be opposed by the Dutch because of their interests but which is not contrary to yours'.[15] Madame may have entrusted this important letter to Verneuil or Courtin to give her brother. She told Charles that her enemies made her suspected on his account. It is astonishing that a Princess, not yet twenty-one, should reveal such marked intelligence, such a flair for politics and diplomacy.

Preoccupied as he was by state affairs, Charles in his loveable way would occasionally include in his correspondence the most intimate little touches: like his Minette he had a delicious sense of humour.

I am very glad to heare that your indisposition of health is turned into a greate belly [he wrote her earlier that winter]; I hope that you will have better lucke with it than the Duchesse [of York] heere had who was brought to bed noonday last of a girle.† I am afraide your shape is not so advantageously made for that convenience as hers is, however a boy will recompense two grunts more, and so good night for feare I fall into naturall philosophy before I thinke of it.

The mass of Englishmen ardently wanted war with the Dutch, though they had no more liking for the French. After receiving a grant from Parliament of £2,500,000, Charles II

* Philip IV.   † The future Queen Anne.

declared war on Holland. When the two new French ambassadors arrived in London they were given a courteous reception by Charles, but it was clear to them that their mission was largely abortive. Courtin noticed the hostility of the people: 'The English,' he informed his friend Lionne the French foreign minister, 'are like their own mastiffs which as soon as they see other dogs throw themselves upon them and throttle them if they can—and then go back home and lie down and go to sleep.'[16]

Minette reveals her desperate anxiety at this time in a letter to Charles towards the end of May:

> According to the latest news from Holland we know that their fleet has come out and that consequently an encounter is certain. This I confess, is a thing which makes me tremble. Whatever advantage you may have, it is after all, Fortune which decides most things in this world....

In his characteristic way, Charles, intending to let his sister see his confidence in his fleet, mentions in the same letter the visit of a valiant soldier, the Maréchal d'Humières, a friend of Turenne's, who was returning to France, and the latest composition of his favourite guitar player, Francesco Corbetta. He was sending it to his sister, hoping it would please her. Charles remained imperturbable and serene.

It was now that the Queen-Mother of France, Anne of Austria fell seriously ill with an acute form of cancer of the breast, and Minette mentions it in a letter to Charles.[17] The King decided to send over a witty, amusing courtier named George Porter, to make inquiries about the Queen-Mother. During his few weeks in France, he certainly succeeded in entertaining the French Court.

Meawhile the malicious pro-Dutch faction at Court were spreading false rumours abroad, that the English fleet had been destroyed, that the Duke of York's ship had been blown up, that the Duke had been drowned, and that King Charles had been compelled to fly from London. La Grande Mademoiselle in her *Mémoires* relates that Madame's acute anxiety made her seriously ill. She was again enciente. Lord Holles wrote to King Charles: 'If things had gone ill at sea, I really believe Madame would have died.' Even if there was a latent antipathy between Madame and the Duke of York—he was jealous of her influence with Charles—the news would have come as a great shock.

Then Charles wrote (6 June) to Minette to give her the glad news that the English fleet under the command of the Lord High Admiral, the Duke of York with Prince Rupert as admiral of the White, and the Earl of Sandwich as Admiral of the Blue had gained a glorious victory over the Dutch at Southwold Bay off Lowestoft. It was the Dutch admiral, Opdam, who had died after a fierce encounter of his flagship the *Eendragt* with *The Royal Charles*.[18] The English losses were comparatively light, but Charles Berkeley (now Earl of Falmouth) an intimate friend of the Duke of York's and two other noblemen had been killed by one cannon shot on the quarterdeck of *Royal Charles*. So close were they to the Duke of York that James was splashed with their blood.

Charles confided to his sister: 'I have had as great a losse as 'tis possible in a good frinde, poore C. Barckeley.'

Monsieur and Madame sent over one of their gentlemen Monsieur de Poullec to England to tell Charles how they rejoiced in his victory. 'Indeed you should be pleased with Monsieur,' wrote Minette to her brother for 'the sentiments he has shown on this occasion and for the manner in which he has declared himself for all that concerns you.'

The Comte de Gramont's courier was the first to bring us the good news yesterday. We were at mass and it caused a great commotion. The King himself cried to his ministers who were in the gallery to rejoice, at which I was greatly surprised, for although in his innermost soul he wishes you all possible success I nevertheless did not think he would have wished to show it publicly because of his engagement with the Dutch.

The Second Dutch War

It is obvious from the tone of Madame's letter that she was pleading with her brother to be content with his victory and to make peace with the Dutch. 'You know how to triumph by clemency as well as by peace,' she assured him. She told Charles that the Comte de Gramont was more English than anybody else. She wondered that he did not get into a thousand scrapes because of it. When alluding to 'the poor Earl of Falmouth', she seems to be trying to influence her brother to make peace. Charles Berkeley would have favoured it, she wrote. However, the victory merely gave Charles and the British people a greater zest to continue the war.

That summer (1665) England was stricken by a terrible plague. When the Court moved to Hampton Court, the French Ambassadors went to Kingston-on-Thames. The Duc de Verneuil wrote home: 'Yesterday I—the Duc de Verneuil—while taking my daily walk along the road, found the body of a man who had died of the plague.'

Queen Henrietta Maria had now returned to France, and she was all the more delighted to be reunited with her favourite daughter. At the end of June, Madame was extremely disconsolate when she gave birth to a still-born daughter, but her mother nursed her devotedly. She made a fairly rapid recovery.

Madame's role as the intermediary between Charles and Louis was now a very delicate one, since her brother was daily growing more irritated and perplexed with the ambiguous attitude of the French King. He was uncertain whether Louis intended to intercede on the side of Holland. Charles needed allies, but the French were not pleased when they heard that the Spanish were intriguing to come to an agreement with Britain. Madame was so concerned that she wrote to her brother arguing against the possibility of an alliance with Spain.

Meanwhile Lord Holles was growing more and more touchy as he revealed in his letters to Sir Henry Bennet. He got on badly with King Louis.

I know [he wrote] the K^g expects a compliment from me as he hath had from the rest of the ambassadors upon the Queens recovery.... It is trew that I had demanded an audience for that purpose as well as they, but was then taken really ill with my greate cold and paine in my hips and made my excuse by Bonnueil and Girant.... I faine would doe for the best, if I could tell, what.[19]

He wrote home that Louis was buying twenty ships from the King of Denmark.

If Cominges was constantly complaining that the London climate did not agree with him, Holles wrote to the Secretary of State of the severe weather of a Paris winter:

The weather, which is here most fierce, a mighty flood upon the melting of the greate snow, and yet every other day a sharpe frost and more snow that men can not worke, especially printers. The flood is so greate that between my house and the Porte St Honoré they goe in boates, a man's height of water in my cellars wch hath spoiled me fifty barrells of beer... severall houses throwen down in the Faubebourg St. Marceau and between 40 and 50 persons drowned.

On 17 September 1665, there came the long-expected death of Philip IV of Spain, and he was succeeded by his sickly son Charles II. By his will Philip had excluded his daughter Marie-Thérèse from the succession. Charles II of Spain was Philip's son by a second marriage, while Marie-Thérèse was his child by a first marriage. Though it was fast declining, Charles II of Spain's Kingdom remained the nucleus of a great empire.[20] Other nations eagerly watched its gradual dissolution. King Louis made a formal claim to the Spanish Netherlands in the name of his wife on the grounds that the Law of Devolution, which applied to those provinces, favoured the children of first marriages rather than those born from second marriages. In his decision to delay hostilities, for the present, Louis was respecting the wishes of his dying mother Anne of Austria to whom he was devoted.

The Second Dutch War

Paris was very gay that winter and Monsieur and Madame gave a magnificent fête at the Palais-Royal. The King attended it, but the Queen was absent owing to mourning, for her father. Louis, dressed in a suit of violet velvet, sparkling with pearls and diamonds, was received by his brother and sister-in-law in the resplendent gallery of the Palais-Royal, aglow with mirrors and illuminated by torches. It has sometimes been alleged that Louis lacked humour, but he was heartily amused by Molière's delightful comedy *Médecin malgré lui* performed that evening on the eve of the Feast of the Three Kings. Whether the Court doctors were as appreciative is another matter. Guy Patin aptly commented: 'So the world laughs at doctors who kill folks with impunity.' The ignorance and conceit of late seventeenth-century physicians were for the most part appalling.

Madame de Motteville, who deeply revered Queen Anne of Austria, relates that on her deathbed the Queen regretted the excessive care she had bestowed on her bodily comfort. It was impossible to find linen of fine enough quality for her underclothing. Anne of Austria died on 20 January 1666 between four and five o'clock in the morning, and the tolling of the great bell of Notre Dame announced her death: Louis wept throughout the night, while Monsieur, crazed with grief, refused to leave her bedside.

'Madame,' he sobbed, 'you have loved me so much here on earth, continue to love me when you will be in heaven and pray God for me.'[21]

'My son, I pray you, leave me in peace,' murmured the dying woman.

To Madame, with whom she had been reconciled she bequeathed the crucifix which she held in her last agony and some valuable jewels. Since they shared the same grief, Louis promised Philippe that his infant son the Duc de Valois would be brought up with the Dauphin. Monsieur and Madame returned for a few days to St. Cloud.

Just before her mother-in-law's death, Minette had informed

109

her brother that Monsieur was writing him a long letter 'to urge you again to a settlement with Holland. For my part,' she told him, 'I confess that I do not care to do things I believe to be useless, so that I content myself with praying to God to inspire you in every way to do what is best.' She informed him of a dramatic event that had lately taken place on the Pont Neuf,* today the oldest bridge in Paris, a duel between a man named La Feuillade and the Chevalier de Clermont.

> on the pretext that Clermont had accused the other of speaking ill of him to the King and Monsieur and had said that he had cheated the Marechal de Gramont at the tables.... The Chevalier de Clermont being the aggressor is convicted of duelling and consequently exiled and the other is safe because witnesses say he did no more than defend himself.[22]

She thought that My Lord St. Albans would be distressed because of 'his love of our friend the Abbé de Clermont'.

Early in the New Year Louis declared war on England, but he made it plain that he was obliged to do so owing to his treaty with Holland. He had little zest for this war, and ordered the Duc de Beaufort, who commanded a squadron of twenty ships to be as dilatory as possible in cooperating with the Dutch fleet in the Channel and the North Sea. Minette and her brother thought it politic to break off their correspondence for some months. The Earl of St. Albans, however, wrote often to Sir Henry Bennet, now Lord Arlington, and kept the minister well appraised as to Madame's state of health. Lord Holles was given three month's grace before having to leave France.

During April, Queen Henrietta Maria intervened in an attempt to mediate between England and Holland. A conference for this purpose was held at St. Germain. Queen Henrietta was present together with her daughter, King Louis, Lord Holles and Monsieur de Lionne. The English ambassador wrote home that the conference was abortive—he described it

---

* The two halves begun in 1578 to the designs of Androuet du Cerceau and completed in 1604.

as '*A Parturiunt Montes*'—The Queen-Mother, he wrote, 'would answer for ye K. her sonne to be ready allwaies to embrace a good peace and for me his servant and minister that I would contribute all that lay in me towards it'.[23]

During the autumn of 1666 there was a marked coldness between King Louis and Madame because of Louise de La Vallière, who was still in high favour with Louis. An unknown correspondent wrote to Sir Philip Frowde during October, in London:

> The Queen of France perceiving Madame de La Vallière big with child hath forbid her to appear before her anymore and disgrac'd some of her ladys of honour who deluded her Majesty that there was nothing but a meere friendship between the King and her.[24]

Marie-Thérèse had objected to Louise de La Vallière attending to her, and Madame apparently had interceded for her sister-in-law. Louis was irritated with Madame and blamed her for the Queen's discovery, though one would have thought that Marie-Thérèse must have been aware of it a long time ago.

Before he finally left France poor Lord Holles was afflicted with gout. 'It is my fate,' he wrote home, 'to have a fitt of the goute at parting as I had at coming and none between.' He was saddened by the death of his wife. He hoped that arrangements might be made to transport him in a yacht from Dieppe to Greenwich because he understood there was much sickness upon the road at Dover, Canterbury and other places.

Lord Holles was to end his career as a Whig opposing the policy of Charles II.

IX

Philippe Falls in Love

Surrounded by his foppish minions, Philippe Duc D'Orléans resembled the Valois King Henri III or even our Edward II. Unfortunately he fell in love with another Philippe, the Chevalier de Lorraine, and Monsieur was weak enough to succumb to his evil influence. It was a friendship that was to cause Madame the deepest distress, though she was such a fine soul that she acquired a subtle understanding of her husband and pitied him with all her heart. However, she was not the type of woman to endure the arrogance and insolence of Philippe's new favourite. Monsieur's second wife Elisabeth Charlotte, Princess Palatine was later to suffer in her turn intolerable affronts from the Chevalier.

Lorraine's contemporaries have found little good to write about this courtier. He was extremely handsome, *'fait comme on peint les anges'* as Choissy described him. Born in 1643, he sprang from a noble family, for he was a younger son of Henri de Lorraine, Comte d'Harcourt. Except for his cherub features he had nothing to recommend him, for he was almost penniless when he came to Court. A godson of Anne of Austria and of Cardinal Mazarin, he soon acquired an absolute mastery over Monsieur's mind. Although Monsieur loaded him with pecuniary favours, he was not even loyal to him. He continued his amorous intrigue with Madame's maid of honour Mademoiselle de Fiennes, and that foolish girl, infatuated with the Chevalier, revealed to him confidential matters concerning the Princess of England. So upset was Monsieur by Lorraine's affair with Mademoiselle de Fiennes that he instructed his confessor Père Zoccoli to warn his favourite that the scandal must cease. So, Henriette D'Angleterre's private life grew increasingly inharmonious, though for a while the sagacious influence of Philippe's friend and grand almoner Daniel de Cosnac was a counter balance to Lorraine. Philippe had once tried to get for Cosnac the Bishopric of Orleans, but he had declined it.

Daniel de Cosnac, Bishop of Valence was a man of great talents, restless, ambitious and for the most part too honest to be a subtle courtier. Madame de Sévigné who knew him well, mentioned that he was so frank of speech and that his temper was so fiery that in conversation with him, it was necessary to be as cautious as when you are driving a shying horse. However, for a while under Cosnac's influence, Philippe d'Orléans reformed his ways. Frivolous and indolent, he even decided to study mathematics. Cosnac counselled Philippe to be prudent wise and secretive. As Philippe was a terrible chatterbox, this was really asking too much. He must, above all, deserve and cultivate the esteem and affection of his brother the King, work diligently to please him, though he must never stoop to flattery. Since Madame had influence with King Louis, it was fitting for Monsieur to make use of this. The King was determined, however, never to allow his brother more power and authority than absolutely necessary. When Monsieur asked his brother for the government of Languedoc, Louis refused his request and Philippe retired in high dudgeon to Villers-Cotterets.

In his absorbing *Mémoires*,[1] Cosnac, who acquired a high opinion of Madame, relates how he was instrumental in serving her on one occasion. Louvois, King Louis's Foreign Minister, no friend of Madame's, had brought to his master's attention a copy of a libellous book entitled *Les Amours du Palais Royal*, printed in Holland. Louis showed it to Madame, and strongly advised her to keep it from Philippe's prying eyes. The libel was the work of Malicorne, a lover of Madame's former resourceful Maid of Honour Mlle. de Montalais. Greatly alarmed, for the details in the book although mainly fictitious, yet bore an air of reality, Madame consulted her friend the Bishop of Valence. He acted with remarkable energy, for he immediately sent a son of the physician Gui Patin to Holland, instructing him to buy up the whole edition of 1800 copies. These were handed over to Monsieur's loyal valet Mérille, and much to Madame's relief burnt in her presence: however, the original copy of the libel somehow escaped destruction. The work has been wrongly attributed to the celebrated author Bussy-Rabatin, who in any case was a friend of Madame's and who would never have stooped to such a despicable act.

According to Cosnac, Madame was inconsolable when her infant son Philippe Charles Duc de Valois died during December 1666 from a feverish cold and convulsions. Monsieur was not much distressed after the first shock. The event was regarded in France as a national disaster since King Louis's only son the Dauphin was a sickly child. He was interred in St. Denis, while his heart was borne to Anne of Austria's Val-de-Grâce. The Prince's governess Suzanne Charlotte de Gramont Madame de St. Chaumont, a sister of the Comte de Gramont and governess to Madame's children was much distressed by the Duc de Valois's death. Princess Henriette was very fond of this lady and she confided in her, revealing her wretchedness after the Chevalier de Lorraine acquired his ascendancy over her husband. Madame de St. Chaumont was not only her devoted friend, but so much her partisan that she provoked the anger and resentment of Monsieur. The household of the Duc and Duchesse d'Orléans seethed with discord and intrigue.

Just before the death of her only son, Madame appeared in the Ballet des Muses as a shepherdess with her crook, holding her inseparable white-and-tan spaniel, Mimi, in her arms. Molière's *Le Sicilien* was the interlude to this ballet. Pierre Mignard was fond of painting Madame together with Mimi. According to Madame de Sévigné, the little spaniel was very jealous when her mistress bestowed her attention on anybody else. Both Minette and Charles were especially fond of spaniels.

During the early months of 1667 Charles II was more ready to listen to King Louis's persuasive diplomacy. By now he was increasingly embarrassed by lack of financial resources, and he agreed to an armistice pending the assembly of a Peace Conference at Breda. The Dutch, however, well aware that Louis was planning to invade the Spanish Netherlands and forseeing an eventual alliance between France and England, refused to agree to an armistice. Their refusal afforded Louis a pretext to free himself from his treaty of obligation with the Dutch and enabled him to open negotiations for a separate peace with Charles II.[2] The tangled webs of Charles's and Louis's diplomatic relations is often confusing, but it is evident that Queen Henrietta Maria and Madame took a part in these secret negotiations. No ministers were entrusted with the secret except for Lionne, Ruvigny the French Ambassador in London, and the Earl of St. Albans closely in the confidence of the old queen Henrietta Maria. Charles promised that he would give no assistance to Spain for a year, while one of his conditions was that the Antilles should be restored to Britain. On his part Louis promised that he would not conduct any alliance against Charles during this period.

The Dutch themselves were divided about whether to continue the war or not, for four of the seven provinces had declared against it. Wanting to revenge the defeats during the previous year, Admiral de Ruyter—a great seaman—cheekily made an attack on Sheerness and Chatham, and succeeded in capturing or destroying more than sixteen British ships. Samuel Pepys wrote in his diary on 12 June: 'Home, where all our hearts do now ake, for the news is true, that the Dutch have broke the chaine and burned our ships, and particularly The Royal Charles.' Actually this fine ship was captured, and *The Royal James* was burned. Many Englishmen shared Pepys's sentiments that it was a national disgrace.

While Louis was preoccupied with his plan to invade the Spanish Netherlands, Monsieur was preening himself that he might become King of Naples. It was but a dream. Had not an astrologer named Perignan read his fate in the stars? Did not his Jesuit Confessor Father Zoccoli say that it was very possible? Monsieur was very superstitious, and sometimes consulted astrologers. Some Neapolitan exiles, who had taken refuge in Paris, visited Philippe to interest him in their projects. Monsieur toyed with the idea, mentioned it to Daniel de Cosnac, Bishop of Valence, but his ardour was quickly cooled when he learnt that Naples was close to Vesuvius and was consequently exposed to the danger of earthquakes.[3]

Louis ordered Marshal Turenne to march to the frontier at the head of an army of 50,000 soldiers. He himself left for Peronne to join his troops and a few days later Monsieur, who was eager to take part in the campaign, arrived there. Before his departure Cosnac had reproached Philippe for his folly, pettiness and uselessness of his life. Now, Cosnac pressed on Monsieur all kinds of advice how he ought to conduct himself as a soldier. He must, above all, never give the impression of boredom. He must create a good impression by his generosity in giving largesse and money to the troops. 'You must be courageous,' he assured him, 'but do not expose your person to too much danger.' Cosnac evidently hoped that a man's life would rid Monsieur of his indolence and effeminacy.

He almost certainly warned him that unless he reformed his ways he would have to leave his service.

Philippe took a theatrical leave of Madame and her ladies, hinting to them that they might never see him again. To the Bishop of Valence he said dramatically, 'Follow me to the camp, and you will see how well I can fight.' He reminded Cosnac that he was a grandson of Henri IV. In all fairness to Monsieur, he was no physical coward, and it was noticed that when he appeared in the trenches at Douay and Tournay he showed sang froid and even valour under fire. When the bellicose Bishop of Valence reached Tournay he accompanied Philippe on his tours of inspection and took steps to see that the Court gazetteers recorded his master's versatility. 'What!' said King Louis one day after he had visited the camp before Tournay, 'do I see M. de Valence in the trenches!' 'Sire,' replied Cosnac, ardently—on this occasion at least he was a courtier—'I have come here to be able to tell others that I have seen the greatest King upon earth exposing his person to the same risks as an ordinary soldier.'⁴ Monsieur took Cosnac's advice and gave presents to some wounded soldier.

The King was by no means gratified to find that his brother had acquired such credit with the troops. He preferred to treat him like a pet poodle. Instead of encouraging him to assert his manhood he only grudgingly gave him any great authority. While Louis was busily conferring with his Marechals de Turenne and Bellefonds, Philippe was left with a crowd of courtesans and subordinate officers in another tent. The quiet Flemish burghers gaped as King Louis's proud armies made triumphal entries into their cities.

Madame remained at St. Cloud, for she was enceinte. She eagerly watched the course of the Campaign, and was overjoyed to hear that her husband had appeared in the trenches. Monsieur, however, was soon bored with the life of a soldier. He found a more congenial occupation in decorating his tent and the hanging of crystal chandeliers. When the Abbé de Clermont arrived bringing the news that Madame was ill, Monsieur was in such a hurry to return to St. Cloud that he omitted to ask his brother's permission to absent himself, despite Cosnac's exhortations that he should do so. Nothing pleased Philippe more than to receive the praise of Madame's ladies. At St. Cloud he found that Madame was dangerously ill as the result of a miscarriage. Philippe wrote King Charles that his sister for a quarter of an hour had been thought by her doctors to be dead.

As soon as Madame had recovered, Monsieur returned to the army and appeared in the trenches at the siege of Lille. There were rumours that he was to receive the post of Lieutenant-General of the Army, and even whispered that the King had promised him the command of an expedition to Catalonia.

King Louis was at Compiegne taking a short respite from his royal duties. With him were his Queen Marie-Thérèse and her ladies, including the arrogant sophisticated Françoise-Athénais de Rochechouart, Marquise de Montespan, who belonged to one of the oldest families in France, soon to become

Louis's new mistress. She was a ravishing brunette, with large blue eyes, who had dyed her hair, for she knew that Louis preferred blondes to brunettes. She made friends with the simple, naïve La Vallière and the stupid Marie-Thérèse calculating that sooner or later she would attract the attention of the King. She was no friend of Madame's, for she was jealous of her influence with King Louis. He had lately created Louise a Duchess, a sure sign Madame thought that he had at last tired of her. When Louise arrived at La Fère she had lost something of her beauty, and had learnt of the Montespan affair. She felt utterly miserable. The arrogant Athénais still unsure of Louis after getting into her carriage said with sickening hypocrisy: 'God preserve me from being the King's mistress.' She appealed to the sensual side of Louis's nature where Louise had appealed to his idyllic and romantic sentiments as a young man. Later, fearing to lose him she resorted to La Voisin and other depraved sorcerers.

Monsieur, too, was feeling elated because his friend the Chevalier de Lorraine suddenly arrived at Tournai. He was so much in love with this disdainful, proud man, that the two young men became inseparable. The soldiers in the trenches made ribald jokes about their friendship. Monsieur, who at first had created quite a good impression, forgot to inspect the sentries and neglected his other duties. Cosnac became more and more uneasy when Philippe and Lorraine remained closeted together at night. He tell us in his *Mémoires* how he tried to influence the Duc d'Orléans to return to the field. It was a fatal friendship and it ruined the remainder of Madame's life. In one engagement the Chevalier was lightly wounded in one of his legs by a grenade, so Philippe fussed about him, like a brooding hen and hardly left his bedside.

Later Monsieur joined his wife at Villers-Cotterets where she had gone with her mother to recuperate after her illness. Much to Cosnac's disgust he wrote to Lorraine every day. Cosnac tried to warn Monsieur against meeting Lorraine his acknowledged favourite. 'You have need of several Chevaliers de Lorraine,' he told Monsieur. Philippe spent his time in rearranging the furniture and the mirrors, a habit that irritated his wife. When the Chevalier arrived at Villers-Cotterets, there was constant discord in the household. Monsieur, much to Madame's disgust, received his favourite with transports of joy. It was now that Lorraine gradually acquired a complete ascendancy over his weak master. He was installed in the best rooms of the Palais-Royal, and became Monsieur's chief confidant.

Madame told Daniel de Cosnac that she was extremely anxious about her husband's infatuation with Philippe de Lorraine. She was frequently closeted with Cosnac, and Monsieur became suspicious and hostile, complaining that she conversed with him too often. He was jealous of her intimate friend Madame de St. Chaumont, her daughter's governess. One day when Monsieur found Cosnac in Madame's apartment, he was very nasty, asking the Bishop of Valence what great secrets had he been discussing with his wife. Under Lorraine's malevolent influence, Monsieur daily grew more hostile to his grand almoner. Madame remonstrated with her husband, telling him that if the Bishop had a fault it was that of serving him with too much zeal and loyalty.

The Bishop of Valence now implored Madame that he might be allowed to resign his office. 'In God's name, Madame,' he told her, 'let me go out honestly by the door, and save Monsieur the trouble of throwing me out of the window!' Philippe, however, soon found a pretext to rid himself of Cosnac. It so happened that he now discovered that his favourite had continued to indulge in a passionate love affair with Mademoiselle de Fiennes, Madame's maid-of-honour. Without informing his wife, he immediately dismissed the girl from her service, telling her to retire to a convent. Meanwhile Madame was naturally mystified why her maid of honour had so abruptly left her employment without her knowledge or consent. Unfortunately Mademoiselle de Fiennes had been indiscreet enough to leave a casket behind her containing more than two hundred letters from the Chevalier to his mistress. Madame handed them over to Cosnac, who sat up for the whole of one night reading them. He was horrified to find that many of the letters contained spiteful references to Madame and even scornful expressions about Monsieur. Cosnac selected a few of the more compromising letters that might be shown the King and Monsieur at some suitable time, thus hoping to ruin Lorraine. The others were returned to Mademoiselle de Fiennes. She immediately warned her lover that some dangerous letters were missing from the casket. Meanwhile Philippe reproached his favourite, and Lorraine in his despicable way, was quite prepared to abandon his mistress at Monsieur's request. Lorraine complained bitterly of Cosnac and succeeded so well in arousing Monsieur's anger against his grand almoner that Monsieur decided to disgrace him. He must sell his office, leave Paris immediately and retire to his diocese. Cosnac naturally appealed to the King, who never much liked him, although he considered him the one man with ability in Philippe's household. Louis sent him a message that he did not actually order him to leave Paris, but he strongly urged him to go in view of his brother's displeasure. Cosnac had enemies in high places such as Colbert and Louvois. For Madame, who had learnt to depend on him, Cosnac's disgrace was a bitter grief, and she reproached herself that she had been responsible.

It is evident that Cosnac, like other contemporaries, felt a deep affection for her. Of all the many eulogies, his was undoubtedly the most true to life and the most sincere. It was written just after he had heard of her death three years later.

Madame had a clear and strong intellect. She was full of good sense, and was gifted with fine perception. Her soul was great and just. She always knew what she ought to do, but did not always act up to her convictions either from natural indolence, or else from a certain contempt for ordinary duties, which formed part of her character. Her whole conversation was filled with a sweetness which made her unlike all other royal personages. It was not that she had less majesty, but she was simpler and touched you more easily, for in spite of her divine qualities she was the most human creature in the world. I have no more to say of this Princess, but that she was the glory and honour of her age, and that this age would have adored her, had it been worthy of her.[5]

Princess Henrietta had a streak of unconventionality, and like other people with noble aims and vision, was impatient of trivialities. As might be expected, Bishop Gilbert Burnet is very critical of the Duchess of Orléans in his work.[6] He was hostile to her religion.

> The King's sister was thought the wittiest woman in France [he wrote]. The King of France had made love to her, with which she was highly incensed, when she saw it was only a pretence to cover his addresses to Madame de La Vallière, one of her maids of honour, whom he afterwards declared openly to be his mistress, yet she had reconciled herself to the King, and was now so entirely trusted by him, that he ordered her to propose an interview with her brother at Dover. . . . The whole conduct of the duchess was calculated to rouse the jealousy of her husband. She fully coincided with the licentious manners of the Parisian Court; was continually involved in amorous intrigues; and so far outraged the decency as to bring with her to England Louise de Keroualle, afterwards Duchess of Portsmouth, for the avowed purpose of influencing her brother by pandering to the passion of which he was most the slave.

Burnet's account is prejudiced and partly inaccurate. He also makes no allowance for some of the evil-disposed people around Madame, who were bent on compromising her. There is also no evidence whatsoever for his bold statement that Henrietta brought her maid of honour Louise de Keroualle to England for the purpose as alleged by the worthy Bishop.

When Minette's friend Frances Stuart, who she had once described to her brother as '*la plus belle fille du monde*', offended the King by eloping with his cousin Charles Stuart, Duke of Richmond and Lennox, Minette tried to intercede for '*La Belle*

Stuart'. King Charles had been passionately in love with Frances, and the girl had flirted outrageously with him, giving him every encouragement, but she almost certainly never became his mistress. Frances married her Duke, and they lived together at his country seat Cobham Hall, near Gravesend.

Charles wrote to Minette from Whitehall on 26 August 1667:

> I do assure you I am very much troubled that I cannot in everything give you that satisfaction I could wish, especially in this business of the Duchess of Richmond wherein you may thinke me ill natured but if you consider how hard a thing 'tis to swallow an injury done by a person I had so much tendérnesse for, you will in some degree excuse the resentment I use towards her.[7]

It was quite a long time before he felt able to forgive her.

Minette was very surprised when her brother dismissed Lord Clarendon from the Chancellorship. He had given such long, faithful service to the Stuarts. She was alarmed about the proceedings in Parliament, and asked Charles for an explanation. Clarendon was very unpopular, and the people blamed him for the sale of Dunkirk to France and for the King's marriage to a childless Queen. Charles had been influenced against him by Lord Arlington, the Duke of Buckingham, Lady Castlemaine and Sir William Coventry. He also had reasons for believing that Clarendon had had a hand in arranging the marriage between Frances Stuart and Richmond. Clarendon took refuge in France, during the autumn of 1667 moving eventually to Rouen, where he completed those glorious historical works for which he is chiefly remembered today. It is evident that Charles resented Clarendon's 'ill conduct in his affairs', and complained that his former minister would try to do him ill offices in France. It is more than possible that Madame interceded with King Louis so that Clarendon might remain in France, for Louis found his presence on French soil somewhat embarrassing. Madame was never afraid of remonstrating with her brother if she did not approve of his policy.

Philippe Falls in Love

The Earl of St. Albans had been requested by Lord Arlington the Secretary of State to use his good offices on his behalf with Madame, for Arlington was aware that King Charles's beloved sister had been prejudiced against him by Buckingham and others. At first Madame certainly did not trust Arlington. In France he was considered pro-Spanish, and he had been envoy at Madrid before the Restoration. The French diplomat Ruvigni called him: '*Espagnol par luimême, et Hollandais par sa femme*', for Isabella van Beverweer was a Dutch woman of noble family. The witty Buckingham mocked Henry Bennet, Lord Arlington for he was very formal and punctilious. St. Albans wrote Arlington during the autumn: 'Madame is in perfect health and great beauty.' In reality Madame was suffering from continual headaches, and her doctors could only think of the remedy of bleeding her. She was sufficiently recovered to take part in the King's hunting parties at Versailles. There she delighted everybody by her prowess as a horsewoman.

In the New Year (1668) Charles II decided to send over to Paris his illegitimate son the Duke of Monmouth.* He was then a strikingly handsome youth of nineteen—only five years younger than his Aunt Minette. Charles was anxious that his son should acquire the polish and elegance of the French Court, and there could be no better mentor than his dear sister. Monmouth arrived in Dieppe from Rye:

> I beleeve you may easily guesse [he wrote] that I am some thing concerned for this bearer James and therefore I put him into your handes to be directed by you in all thinges, and pray use that authority over him, as you ought to do in kindnesse to me.

Madame, partly for her brother's sake, treated the graceful Monmouth with the greatest kindness, gave some balls and fêtes in his honour in the Palais-Royal and got on extremely well with him. In return Monmouth taught his aunt the English country dances, so much in vogue at her brother's Court in

* By Lucy Walter his Welsh mistress.

123

Whitehall. The Abbe de Choisy relates in his *Mémoires*[8] that Madame took care to order the most magnificent clothes for Monmouth. She grew to love him for himself, and his gaiety and graceful manners often reminded her of her brother.

So often was Madame closeted with her nephew, that he aroused the jealousy of Monsieur, and the odious Lorraine was only too ready to fan the flames of Monsieur's anger. Some even suspected that there was a liaison between them. The Abbe de Choisy did not think so; there was between them, he wrote, *'une sorte de Jargon'*. It is all too easy to suspect people who are naturally attentive to one another. Monsieur complained to his wife that she talked English with Monmouth though that was natural enough. She complained of the Chevalier's insolence, and that he was attempting to rule her household.

Madame confided in her daughter's governess Madame de St. Chaumont, who sought an interview with King Louis. Although the King of France was censorious about his brother's behaviour to Madame, he really did not mind too much so long as Philippe d'Orléans was not asserting himself or showing any ability as a soldier. However, he reproached Monsieur, who by way of revenge carried his wife off to Villers-Cotterets. A blanket of snow lay over the vast forests, and Madame was forced to endure her husband's and Lorraine's detested society.

Madame missed Daniel de Cosnac. She had written to him when he was first compelled to leave the Palais-Royal.

I hope that you will regard these events as a trick of destiny, which is not to be resisted, and understand that the fatality which has cost you Monsieur's favour, does not extend to me, for I shall ever retain the same esteem I have always felt for you, and shall do my utmost to prove this by my actions.[9]

X

Madame's Interest in Literature and Drama

It may be little known, but Madame was keenly interested in literature and drama, and her exalted position gave her every opportunity to encourage and inspire Molière, Racine, La Fontaine and Boileau in their work. Molière, whose chief patron was Louis XIV himself, dedicated his play *L'École des Femmes* (published in 1662) to Madame.

In his dedication he wrote of 'that charming sweetness (*douceur*) with which you temper the pride of your exalted rank, of that winning kindness, that generous affability which you show to all the world'. Princess Henriette was a discriminating, intelligent judge of French literature. She was generous, too, in her support of the great dramatist when his play *Tartuffe* was fiercely criticized by the priests. Monsieur was the official protector of Molière's Company of actors, and a private performance of this play was given in his house during July 1664, before King Louis, Queen Marie-Thérèse and the Queen-Mother. Madame constantly implored King Louis to licence it publicly and arranged for a special performance of *Tartuffe* to be played before the King at Villers-Cotterets. When it was later performed during August, 1667, it played to a packed house, but M. de Lamoignan, Président du Parlement acting as Home Secretary in the absence of the King decided to ban *Tartuffe*. Madame sent one of her gentlemen to protest to Lamoignan, but it was to no avail.[1] The King thought highly of Molière, and liked the play, but justified the prohibition on the grounds that a comedy which attacked hypocrisy might be construed as an attack upon genuine piety. The royal licence was not finally granted until February 1669.

When Molière was being attacked by his enemies and criticized for his play *Le Misanthrope*, considered by some the finest of his works, Madame gave the dramatist her generous sympathy and understanding.* She at once appreciated its truth and power. She, too, like its author, hated pretence and hypocrisy.

The Abbé Bossuet, too, in his famous *Oraison* praises Madame for her 'excellent judgement in art and letters, which made all those who succeeded in pleasing Madame feel satisfied that they had attained perfection'. The quality that most appealed to Bossuet in Madame was what he described as her 'incomparable douceur'—that sweetness and gentleness so much a part of her character. In an immortal phrase Bossuet said in his *Oraison*: '*Oui, Madame fut douce envers la mort, comme elle l'était envers tout le monde.*' It is a lovely phrase that somehow lingers in the memory.

It was Madame, who persuaded her intimate friend Marie-Madeleine de La Fayette to write her *Madame Henriette d'Angleterre*. One day in her garden at St. Cloud, the Princess told her friend the story of de Guiche's love for her.

There was a child-like quality about Henriette, the radiant smile that lit up her face when she was amused. She now suggested that her friend, who was such an accomplished story teller, should write a novel about her life. What makes this book especially interesting is that Madame read much of Marie-Madeleine's work together with her friend. She would laugh merrily and discuss the difficulties of the venture with Madame de La Fayette.

The element that gave Madame most pleasure was water. From childhood she had always loved it, listening entranced to the music of fountains at Colombes, or the mocking murmur of streams flowing through woodlands. It was as if something in her nature had an affinity with this element. She loved to bathe in fresh, sparkling water, though Dr. Esprit warned her against

* Julia Cartwright Madame Henriette Duchess of Orléans.

it. It enchanted her to sail in the gaily coloured barge that Charles had given her to the sound of Lulli's violins.

Her longing to see her brother only intensified with the years, and she thought wistfully of the seas and of English ships, so dear to his heart.

It was a relief to sublimate her impulses and longings, so she did not spare herself in her generous appreciation of the works of men of genius. Jean Racine owed much to Madame when writing his early tragedies. Renowned for her sensibility and intelligence, she at once perceived that Racine had great talent. Where admirers of his older rival Corneille scoffed at him, she gave him her constant support in his early career:[2] so it was fitting that Racine should dedicate his third tragedy *Andromaque* to her during November 1667, first performed in the Queen's apartments in the Louvre. It is evident that she had allowed him to read to her parts of the play, and had even made constructive suggestions. The play was inspired by a short passage in *The Aeneid* which describes the captive Andromache weeping before Hector's cenotaph. In his dedication Racine wrote:

> They may condemn my *Andromaque* as much as they will, now I can appeal from the subtleties of their imagining, to the heart of your Royal Highness. But, Madame, I know that you judge the merits of a work, not alone by the heart but by the light of an intellect that cannot be deceived.

When first performed the play was a triumphant success.

It was Madame, who suggested the subject of a new tragedy to Racine Bérénice, Queen of Judea is in love with the Emperor Titus, but for reasons of state he is compelled to renounce her and she returns broken-hearted to her country. It is probable that Racine had Princess Henrietta partly in mind in his subtle-delineation of the character of Bérénice. Bérénice reminds one of Henrietta in her tenderness, her gentleness and in her moods of resignation. The Emperor Titus may be modelled on Louis, who had been forced by reasons of state to renounce his early love Marie Mancini. Is it possible that Racine was recalling her reproachful often-quoted words? 'You are the King, you weep, and I am going away.' Marie Mancini was of a passionate nature, and Racine when writing his tragedy may have thought of the grand renunciation. It was with a sense of challenge that Madame watched the rivalry between Corneille and Racine. The younger dramatist was at first unaware that Madame had suggested the same idea to Corneille, but Racine's *Bérénice* was first performed on 21 November 1670, and Corneille's *Tite et Bérénice* was played at the Palais-Royal a week later.

It is surely tragic that Madame had died a few months before in rather mysterious circumstances.

Julia Cartwright relates in her Life of *Madame* a charming anecdote about Madame and the poet Boileau, revealing as it does the streak of unconventionality latent in her nature. Madame much liked his poem *Le Lutrin*, inspired, it is said, by a quarrel as to the removal of an old reading-desk in the choir of the Sainte-Chapelle. One day when following the King and Queen to mass, in the chapel of Versailles, she happened to notice the poet among a group of courtiers. She beckoned to Boileau to approach, and breathed in his ear:

*Soupire, étand les bras, ferme l'oeil et s'en dort**

Her kindly act, so graceful and spontaneous, was widely noticed and very beneficial to Boileau's early career.

Another poet well known to Madame was Jean de La Fontaine, and he wrote *The Epithalamium* in her honour. Madame de La Fayette had almost certainly introduced La Fontaine to Madame. She was familiar with his *Contes* (1665), and his *Fables*, which were published in 1668.

La Fontaine was nicknamed 'Le Bonhomme' or 'Goodman La Fontaine'. In his study of the human race he showed keen insight, but he was hopelessly impractical in his own affairs. A loose liver he was, however, an excellent moralist.

Roger de Rabatin, Comte de Bussy, an author known for his mordant wit—he was a cousin of Madame de Sévigné—

***

* Sigh, stretch your arms, close your eye, and sleep.

had the misfortune owing to his impudence and sarcasm to offend the King. As he was on friendly terms with Madame, Bussy implored her to intercede for him with the King. This she did to good purpose, for Bussy was pardoned and allowed to retain his post at Court, provided he promised to amend his behaviour. Later Louvois the Foreign Minister told Bussy that somebody had accused him of speaking badly about Madame to the King. 'Why,' he protested, 'she is the best of my friends, if I may venture to speak in such a manner of so exalted a lady.'

Bussy was very fond of Madame and very grateful to her for interceding for him.

> I was as much obliged to Madame [he wrote in his *Mémoires*] as If she had saved my life, and although I knew she had a natural disposition to do good to everyone, yet the honour she did me, and the manner in which she treated me, made me think that she worked with more zeal for me than for others. To tell the truth, she saw that I was much attracted to her, and greatly admired her good qualities for she was, both in mind and person, the most charming princess that ever lived.

He was to write after her death to Madame de Scudery

> I am in agreement with you that she had more goodness and more delicacy in her spirit than all the women at Court and virtuous people will miss her extremely.[3]

Bussy was constantly in trouble, for he was imprisoned in the Bastille during April 1665, and later exiled to his native Burgundy.

Another of Madame's friends was the distinguished scholar Monsieur de Tréville, who held the post of Captain of the Musketeers in Monsieur's household. He was reputed to be the best scholar at Court, a man, who fell in love with Madame, although his sentiments were almost certainly platonic. Bishop Burnet, who got to know Tréville very well after Madame's

death, wrote that the Princess had an intrigue with him. He
wrote:[4]

> When she was in her agony, she said 'Adieu Treville'. He
> was so struck with this accident, that it had a good effect on
> him, for he went and lived many years among the fathers
> of the Oratory.... He was a man of a very sweet temper,
> only a little too formal for a Frenchman.... He hated the
> Jesuits and had a very mean opinion of the King....

Henri de La Tour d'Auvergne Vicomte de Turenne, one of
France's greatest soldiers, was also very attached to Madame
and sometimes visited her in St. Cloud. As he grew older, his
mind turned increasingly to religion. Formerly a strong Calvin-
ist he turned Catholic in 1667, but his motives for doing so were
probably genuine, though he has been accused of wanting
merely to curry favour with King Louis. Turenne was intimate
with people in Madame de Sévigné's circle, and although
naturally shy and modest, enjoyed Madame's society.

Madame has been compared with her own great-grandmother
Mary Queen of Scots, and indeed she possessed all the romantic
charm of Mary Stuart, her grace and literary culture, and, above
all, both royal ladies had the gift of fascinating all hearts. In
their private lives they were capable of behaving indiscreetly.
Madame, however, had far more intelligence than her great-
grandmother, and a real flair and zest for politics not possessed
by Mary Queen of Scots.

There is a certain resemblance between Madame and her
own grand-daughter, the lively and enchanting Marie Adélaïde de Savoie, Duchesse de Bourgogne.[5] The resemblance is
a superficial one, for Princess Henrietta Anne had far more
character. There was a serious aspect to her character certainly
lacking in the frivolous and self-indulgent Marie-Adélaïde. She
was disgracefully spoilt by King Louis, who pampered her
every whim. With her zest for pleasure Marie-Adélaïde can be
more justly compared with Queen Marie-Antoinette.

XI

Preliminary Negotiations

During the late summer (1667), King Louis proposed terms of peace to Spain, but the Spaniards procrastinated. This exasperated Louis, so during the winter, though the season was not suitable for a campaign, he invaded Franche Comté, the Spanish possession on France's eastern frontier. The King was soon able to annex the whole province.

Louis's conquest made Charles II in England distinctly uneasy. Together with Lord Arlington he now decided to send over Sir William Temple, the most able diplomat of his age and very much liked by the Dutch, to Holland to negotiate an offensive and defensive alliance with that nation. He had been trained by Arlington. The formation of what is known in history as the Triple Alliance was an attempt to redress the Balance of Power. It was signed by Britain and Holland on 23 January 1668, and it was later joined by Sweden, the most powerful of the Scandinavian states in May 1668. Sir William Temple soon discovered that Jan de Witt, Grand Pensionary of the United Provinces of Holland, had discussed the whole matter with M. Puffendorff a Swedish agent, recently arrived from Paris. The French had done their utmost he told him, to deter the Swedes from giving their formal adherence to the alliance, stating that the English would certainly fail them. There were those, like the rising politician, Sir Thomas Clifford, who heartily disliked the Dutch alliance. 'For all this joy we must soon have another war with Holland,' he remarked.[1]

It was a masterly stroke on the part of Charles to initiate the Triple Alliance, but King Louis had every right to protest, since the Treaty was a violation of the secret agreement made

131

between the two Kings in April 1667. One can but marvel at Charles's subtlety, and cleverness in the mazes of European politics. He understood foreign politics better than any of his ministers. His travels in his early manhood had been of great advantage to him. He knew the inside of a Frenchman's mind, like a book. Extremely intelligent, he lacked political morality. He was a cynical opportunist and believed that the ends justified the means. His real ultimate objective was an intimate alliance with France. It was necessary to achieve this for he was an admirer of the French monarchy, for he, too, longed for unrestrained power. He distrusted the House of Commons and resented their interference. In three matters he was completely sincere, his love for Minette, his devotion to the British navy and his realization that sea-power was of vital importance to England.

Minette was naturally concerned that her brother should make a treaty with Holland, and wrote him asking for an explanation. He tried to justify his attitude:

> I believe you will be a little surprised [he wrote] at the Treaty I have concluded with the States, the effect of it is to bring Spaine to consent to the peace upon the termes the King of France hath avowed he will be content with, so I have done nothing to prejudice France in this agreement and they cannot wonder that I provide for my selfe against any mischief this warr may produce, and finding my propositions to France receave so cold an answer which in effect was as good as a refusall, I thought I had no other way but this to secure myselfe.[2]

Minette had written to him, hoping that he had been reconciled with Frances Stuart Duchess of Richmond, but Charles for the present could not forgive her. In the same letter he told Minette:

> if you were as well acquainted with a little fantasticall gentleman calld cupide as I am, you would neither wonder nor

take ill any sudden changes ... but in this matter there is nothing done in it.

However, when the lady was smitten with smallpox, Charles's old feelings for her again stirred in him, and on her recovery she received him in her house. So engrossed was he in conversation with her that he even missed the post to Minette.

About this time Sir John Trevor was sent by Charles to Paris to propose terms of mediation between France and Spain. Eventually on 22 April 1668, the peace of Aix-La-Chapelle was negotiated. Louis agreed to surrender his newly annexed province of Franche Comté, provided he retained the towns of Spanish Flanders acquired during the previous campaign. Trevor evidently at first offended Madame, for she complained to her brother, who chided the diplomat 'for carrying himselfe so like an asse to you, it was a faute for want of good breeding which is a disease very much spread over this country', he told her. Trevor was more careful to acquire Madame's good opinion. He supported her when she used her influence at the French Court to prevent Lord Clarendon being expelled from France.

It is most unfortunate that several of Minette's important letters to her brother have been lost or destroyed, for instance one written on 7 March 1668 in which she maintains that Charles had been persuaded by his ministers into the Triple Alliance against his better judgement. Indeed Charles was very sensitive about this matter, constantly telling his sister that he was master in his own Kingdom and that she must inform Louis that he was not ruled by Buckingham, Arlington or any other of his ministers. He gave an impression of indolence, but his many visits, to shipyards at Chatham and Portsmouth reveal his energy when his interest was aroused.

Charles's reaction to scandals in France is usually delightful, for he watched events from France with keen relish. When the beautiful Hortense Mancini, Duchesse de Mazarin, soon to take up residence in England, fled from her husband, who was almost insanely jealous of her, Charles comments: 'I see wives do not love devoute husbands, which reason this woman had besides many more as I heare to be rid of her husband upon any termes', or in another letter his delicious remark: 'I am sorry to finde that cucolds in France grow so troublesome, they have been inconvenient in all countries this last yeare.' The little personal touches are, too, most pleasing. When Monmouth was about to return to Paris, he ends one letter to Minette by telling her: 'He intends to put on a perriwig againe when he comes to Paris, but I beleeve you will thinke him better as I do with his short haire.' On one occasion Monmouth, who was most unreliable, lost or mislaid a letter in French King Charles had given him intended for Monsieur. Charles said in his cynical way that a man who could lose his credentials bode fair to become a good ambassador in time. Monmouth was inclined to be thoughtless and when he returned to England omitted to thank his Aunt Henriette for all her kindness to him. Charles told his sister that he feared that his son took after him in being an indifferent letter writer.

During the spring (1668) Charles was so anxious about Minette's health that he sent his own physician Dr. Alexander Fraizer to France to attend her. After she had recovered from a serious illness, her devoted mother said that it was entirely due to a Mass she had said on her behalf. Charles privately thought that her recovery was aided by Sir Theodore Mayerne's pills. These had been prescribed by Dr. Fraizer. 'For God's Sake,' he implored her, 'have a care of your diett and beleeve the planer your diett is the better health you will have. Above all have a care of strong brothes and gravy in the morning. . . .'

On 18 July 1668 a magnificent fête was given by King Louis at Versailles. Ostensibly it was to celebrate the peace of Aix-La-Chapelle, but it also represented the triumph of Louis's mistress Madame de Montespan. The lovely gardens were now open to the public for the first time. Madame was there, and three hundred ladies were the King's favoured guests at his table. The orangery with its exotic birds from Asia and Africa was a great attraction. Molière's new play, *Georges Dandin* was performed on this occasion, and the audience were richly amused at the antics of the wretched cuckold, who reminded them of M. de Montespan. Madame de Sévigné, who was present, has described the splendour, the music by Lulli, the dancing under the trees, and the magnificent display of fireworks. Monmouth danced with Madame—they were both superb dancers—in a bosquet open to the sky where there were orange trees skilfully arranged in silver tubs. Monsieur could not conceal his jealousy. King Charles eagerly awaited the return of the Duke of Monmouth, who was among the guests, to hear an account of the fête.

During the summer King Louis decided to send another ambassador to London. He chose Colbert de Croissy,* an accomplished diplomat. He was younger brother of the King's minister. Louis was now just as eager for an alliance with England as Charles was to make progress with the negotiations with Louis. Colbert de Croissy arrived on 19 August, a comely man in a black suit. Evelyn had never seen a richer coach. It is evident that he was not much trusted either by Charles or Arlington, though Charles was well satisfied with him at first. There was even some talk of having him recalled. Ralph Montague, who was appointed British ambassador in France during the summer of 1668, did not actually take up his post in France until the spring (1669). Madame later told Ralph Montagu that the French thought it a great compliment to send Colbert de Croissy to London, particularly as he was the chief minister's brother. Because Colbert de Croissy possessed great credit in France, she tactfully told Montagu that she was not willing to interfere in trying to get him recalled for fear of displeasing the French king.[3]

During the whole of 1668, Madame was incessantly grieved by her husband's infatuation for the Chevalier de Lorraine. Occasionally Monsieur was a little kinder to her, but his customary attitude was one of grudging and sulky suspicion.

* Charles, Marquis de Croissy et de Torcy (1625–96).

135

Charles refers to Monsieur's better mood in his letter of 9 August:

> I am very glad [he wrote] that Monsieur begins to be ashamed of his rediculous fancyes. You ought undoutedly to oversee what is past so that for the future he will leave being of those fantasticall humours ... For his friend the Chevalier I thinke you have taken a very good resolution not to live so with him but that when there offers a good occasion, you may ease your selfe of such a rival....

The Abbé de Choisy relates in his *Mémoires*[4] an incident relating to a chivalrous adventurer the Chevalier Louis de Rohan and Madame. His vanity made him believe, wrote the Abbé, that Madame would be grateful if he took upon himself the role of avenger of her wrongs. Much to Madame's embarrassment, the Chevalier de Rohan picked a violent quarrel with the Chevalier de Lorraine and struck him in the presence of witnesses. The matter seemed very nasty: Madame complained to King Louis, who ordered the Duc de Noalles to investigate the affair. Louis de Rohan was forced to apologize, though he assured ten of his friends in writing that he had only done so to avoid being punished, under the edicts against duelling. Minette mentioned the affair to Charles in one of her letters. He alludes to it in his letter of 27 December:

> I am very glad that the Chevalier de Rohan has that mortification put upon him by your desire, for it will make others have a care of there behaviour towards you....

Minette was again enceinte, and Charles had to admit that he regretted it had to come at this time when he was planning the secret negotiations in which his sister was to play such a vital part. It is clear that Charles already had in mind that his sister should visit him in England. During his first interviews with Colbert de Croissy, the ambassador was left in no doubt of Madame's influence with her brother and how highly he thought of her. Charles made it clear to the ambassador that a treaty of commerce must precede the negotiations for an alliance in which England's maritime interests were safeguarded. Where the naval interests of great Britain were concerned, Charles's attitude was altogether uncompromising. He never feared France's military power on the continent, but he jealously regarded Louis's attempts to build a powerful fleet and to extend her sea-borne commerce, as he told his sister on 2 September:

> The great applycation there is at this time in France to establish trade and to be very considerable at sea, which is so jealous a point to us heere who can be only considerable by our trade and power by sea, as any stcps that France makes that way must continue a jealousy betweene the two nations which will upon all occasions be a great hinderance to our intire friendship....

Colbert de Croissy perceived this quite clearly when he wrote to his Foreign Minister on 19 January 1670.[5] 'I am very much afraid that the command of the Fleet and the etiquette of flags and salutes will be an inviolable and perpetual obstacle to the desired alliance.'

Puffed with vanity and the ardent desire to stay in Madame's good graces, George Villiers Duke of Buckingham approached the French ambassador through his friend Sir Ellis Leighton with tentative proposals intended to bring about an alliance with France. Acting independently of Buckingham, Lord Arlington the Secretary of State also made overtures to Colbert de Croissy through Sir Joseph Williamson with a similar object. Arlington was not considered sincere in France, for he was thought to be either pro-Dutch or pro-Spanish. It was later very difficult to rid Madame's mind of a strong prejudice against Arlington. Buckingham sent Sir Ellis Leighton on a special mission to Madame, charging him to tell her how ardently he desired an alliance between the two countries. Dryden has described the brilliant clown Buckingham in immortal verse:

> But in the course of one revolving moon,
> was chymist, fiddler, statesman and buffoon,
> Then all for women, panting, rhyming, drinking,
> Besides ten thousand freaks that died in thinking.

King Charles watched Buckingham's activities in the political sphere with rich, sardonic amusement. He was now fully engaged in secret negotiations with his sister, and, though he liked Buckingham's society, had no intention whatsoever of confiding in him the main secret. Indeed he was always stressing to Minette the necessity of absolute secrecy in their correspondence. For this purpose he now wished to send her a cypher. On one occasion an unknown Italian handed Charles a confidential letter from Madame in a dark passage, so that it was impossible to recognize his face. Charles later told Minette that he intended to prorogue Parliament from 1 March 1669 until 19 October.

It is evident that neither Colbert de Croissy nor Ralph Montagu who was soon to leave for France as British ambassador, were admitted into what Charles called 'The Great Secret'. Louis fully trusted his ambassador, but Charles was strongly opposed to confiding in Colbert de Croissy until a much later stage in the negotiations. Charles never fully trusted even Arlington with the entire secret. As for the French ministers, Lionne and Louvois knew as much as anybody, and Marshal de Turenne was later consulted concerning various military matters.

Briefly, it was later proposed during the summer (1669) that Charles should agree to join Louis in a premeditated invasion of Holland. Provided he was prepared to cooperate with the King of France's forces both by sea and land, Louis on his side would agree to give him large yearly subsidies as long as the war lasted and an ultimate share in the spoils of the conquered provinces after the allied powers had conquered Holland.

Influenced by his sister and old mother, and perhaps by his

wife, all devoted Roman Catholics, Charles's sympathies inclined towards Roman Catholicism. He could not forget that some of his most loyal supporters were members of that religion, particularly those who had given him shelter and indeed saved him from his enemies after the Battle of Worcester. He intended therefore when a favourable condition existed to make a public declaration that he was a Roman Catholic and to enlist the aid of France for this purpose. Fully aware of the state of feeling and prejudice against Roman Catholicism in England, Charles was far too much a political realist to make this declaration unless he could feel absolutely secure in his kingdom. Whatever else happened, he was determined never to go on his travels again. Whether or not Charles was sincere in his intention to declare himself a Roman Catholic at this juncture is a difficult matter to determine. If he could have achieved it without the grave risk of losing his throne or indeed total ruin, Charles might have taken this momentous step in early 1669 or later and not left his ultimate conversion to his deathbed in February 1685. Charles admired Louis's absolute monarchy and favoured it, if that were possible in his own kingdom. Even Minette, who was fully apprized as to the secret negotiations, was convinced that her beloved brother was sincere in his intended conversion, but Charles played his hand with cool insouciance, confiding fully in nobody.

XII

'The Great Secret'

It was James Duke of York, who advised his brother to summon to a secret meeting various trusted councillors to whom he could safely confide his thoughts on matters of religion. This important meeting was held on 25 January 1669 in the Duke's closet, and besides the King there were present the Duke of York, Lord Arlington, Sir Thomas Clifford and Henry Third Lord Arundell of Wardour.

Charles now told these counsellors that he had called them together to advise him about ways and means to be devised to advance the cause of Catholicism in his kingdom and to consider the possibility that he might publicly declare himself a Catholic at the most proper time.

The Duke of York was at this period secretly a Catholic, but neither Arlington nor Clifford were then members of that church. Though he favoured toleration, Arlington was not a religious man, but Clifford on the other hand was deeply religious by temperament. Like Charles's sister, Clifford was a Devon man and his family seat was at Ugbooke, near Chudleigh in Devon. He has been aptly described by Sir Arthur Bryant as a Restoration Strafford—'heroic, passionate and reckless . . . rugged and tempestuous as the Dartmoor from which his ancient race sprang'.[1] His contemporary John Evelyn described him as 'a valiant uncorrupt gentleman, ambitious not covetous, generous, passionate, a most constant sincere friend to me in particular'. Nobody played a more vital part during the negotiations preceding the Treaty of Dover. If there was a rough core to his nature, he was honest and kindly, though his great fault was his inflexibility.

Lord Arundell was a professed Roman Catholic, a man

known for his loyalty to the Stuarts. He had fought during the Civil War, and now held the office of Master of the Horse to Queen Henrietta Maria. He was a keen gambler and sportsman. Charles wisely chose him to carry over proposals for an alliance with Louis. Although no trained diplomatist, it was of advantage to him that in his capacity as the Queen-Mother's Master of the Horse, he had plausible excuses for visiting the Queen in France.

Meanwhile Ralph Montagu the new British Ambassador, then aged thirty-one, who already knew Madame quite well, had taken up his duties in Paris. Montagu tactfully decided that the awkward question of the precedence of coaches would present few problems to him, since he was prepared to order it for the best, according to Madame's advice and directions, 'who understands all these things extremely well and is in all points that concerne the King's (Charles II's) Honor equally concerned with Himself'. Madame, however, was at first prejudiced against Montagu, for she considered him Lord Arlington's man. 'She told the King of France, according to the Ambassador, there was no good to be expected from me, for I was sent hither to do just as you pleased and directed.'[2] For my Lord Buckingham she durst almost answer for,' wrote Montagu to Lord Arlington. When a rising politician Sidney Godolphin visited Madame he praised Arlington as much as possible, but the Secretary of State's enemies in France had damaged her opinion of him. Maréchal de Turenne had taken Mr. Godolphin aside to say how well Arlington deserved everybody's good will.[3]

Montagu was an accomplished diplomat well suited to his Paris post, and he formed a high opinion of Madame. 'Madame', he wrote to Arlington, is in everything extremely concerned for the King my master's interest and with a great deal of address and discretion.'

Charged with his mission to King Louis, Lord Arundell arrived in France at the beginning of March, accompanied by Sir Richard Bellings, a Catholic gentleman, who was reputed to be one of the best French scholars in England. Arundell was required by Charles to inform Louis of his intention to make a public avowal of the Roman Catholic religion, and to request Louis to provide him with money and troops in case they were necessary. Charles informed Madame of Arundell's impending arrival in France, making use of a cypher for the first time.

The correspondence of Colbert de Croissy is fascinating. He mentions the Abbé Pregnani, an Italian Theatine monk, a fashionable dabbler in astrology. Monmouth, who was very superstitious, had been impressed by the Abbé, and was eager that he should visit his father's Court in England. Louis had the humorous notion of using the garrulous Pregnani as a sort of unofficial agent and spy. He was instructed to make astrological predictions showing the great benefits to be gained from an alliance with France.[4] When he arrived in England, the Abbé saw Colbert de Croissy and asked him to instruct the Duke of Monmouth with various matters to say to King Charles, designed to influence him to bring about without hesitation a strict alliance 'with the King our masters'.[5]

Charles was far too shrewd to be deceived by these manœuvres. Although he found Pregnani's conversation amusing, he did not take him seriously. He wrote to Minette on 7 March:

> I had almost forgott to tell you that I find your friend L'Abbé Pregnany a man very ingenious in all things I have talked with him upon, and I find him to have a greate deale of witt but you may be sure I will enter no further with him than according to your carrecter.

The King enjoyed the bracing air at Newmarket where he invited the Abbé to see the horse races. 'He was so uneasy with riding from Audley End hither to see the foot match, as he is scarce recovered yett,' he told his sister. Charles was richly amused when the credulous Monmouth lost his money because he followed Pregnani's wrong predictions.

Charles returned to Whitehall and wrote to his sister on 22

142

March in cypher* (it was the same letter in which Charles mentions Monmouth's ill luck).

> 341 [Buckingham] knowes nothing of 360 [Charles II] intentions towards 290. 315 Catholic Religion nor of the person 334 [Charles II] sends to 100 [Louis XIV] and you need not feare that 341 [Buckingham] will take it ill that 103 [Madame] does not write to him, for I have toald him that I have forbid 129 [Madame] to do it for feare of intercepting of letters.

Charles was anxious to conceal from Buckingham, who was a Protestant, and St. Albans the proposed secret clauses relating to religion, although he was fully aware of the political negotiations.

It is very diverting to see how cleverly Charles and Madame succeeded in hoodwinking Buckingham, and even St. Albans. However, by January 1669 Buckingham heard through his sister Mary Villiers Duchess Dowager of Richmond, who was in attendance on Queen Henrietta Maria, that Madame and Louis were frequently engaged in important consultations at Colombes. Buckingham was much piqued, feeling that he was being deceived. He complained to his friend Sir Ellis Leighton, who warned Madame of the Duke's indignation. The Princess with her customary tact attempted to appease Buckingham, for she wrote to Sir Ellis Leighton in flattering terms about the Duke, though in a very depreciatory way about his rival Arlington. 'The attachment of this man to the Dutch being too ... evident and his inclination and partiality for Spain too well known', she wrote to Leighton.[6] Madame most adroitly concealed from Buckingham that she herself was engrossed in secret negotiations with Charles. Buckingham, who was notorious for his affairs with women, adored Madame, though she did not give him the slightest encouragement. When Buckingham returned to London, and the Abbé Pregnani brought him no message from Madame on official business, the Duke was deeply hurt.

* The Key to the Cypher is preserved in the French Archives.

He assured her that she had absolute power to make him obey her in all things. 'I am in despair', he wrote her, 'at finding myself always in danger of passing for a rascal or a visionary through the eagerness and mistakes of certain people who do not understand our business.'[7] Perhaps he was referring to Arlington among others now high in Charles's favour.

One messenger used by King Charles to carry over a letter containing nothing confidential to Minette was John Wilmot Second Earl of Rochester, a poet of genius and author of that lovely lyric 'Absent from thee I languish still'. He was son of the King's companion in his escape after Worcester. Charles wrote:

> This bearer, my Lord Rochester, has a mind to make a little journey to Paris, and would not kiss your hands without a letter from me ... you will find him not to want wit and did behave himself, in all the Dutch war, as well as anybody, as a volunteer.[8]

It was Ralph Montagu, who conceived a very ingenious scheme to reconcile Madame to Arlington. Montagu was well aware Monsieur's allowance to his wife for her household was a niggardly £3,000 a year. He now wrote to his sister Lady Harvey, a lady of some influence at the English Court, suggesting that Lord Arlington might persuade King Charles to give his sister a considerable sum of money, for she was very hard up. King Louis no longer gave her the presents of money he used to give her. Montagu suggested that the money could be made available from the remainder of Queen Catherine of Braganza's portion, for Sir Robert Southwell, a former ambassador in Portugal, had succeeded in obtaining a promise that it would be paid. Surely £5,000 could be spared as a present to Madame.

When the Princess heard from Montagu that Arlington had been instrumental in obtaining her the money, Montagu wrote to Lady Harvey:

> She was a little surprised and out of countenance at the thing, but you never saw anybody take anything more kindly, both

of the King and Lord Arlington. She is extremely afraid lest
her mother, or husband should know anything of it and
desires that it may be the greatest secret in the world.[9]

Montagu thought that King Charles would do well to save
the charges of an ambassador and give Madame the money,
for Monsieur 'spends all a back way upon the Chevalier de
Lorraine'.

Madame gave splendid service to her brother-in-law Louis
acting as intermediary between him and Charles, but Montagu
told Arlington, that she was 'truly and passionately concerned
for the King and brother'. Henriette's sympathies might be to
some extent French, but she had a profound affection for England. Not only Ralph Montagu's correspondence, but the Clifford Mss reveal quite clearly that Madame would never have
been willing to sacrifice England to the interests of France. What
she lacked was a subtle understanding of the real sentiments
of the people of England, hardly to be expected considering
the limited range of her sojourns in her native country. Arlington had done her a pecuniary favour and in gratitude she
warned Montagu in early September that Colbert de Croissy had
been given orders to stir up trouble with the Parliament and
to compass Arlington's ruin, if that were possible. Montagu
wrote Arlington:

> You may give credit to Madame's intelligence, for some of
> the most understanding people of France apply themselves to
> Madame, having a great opinion of her discretion and judge-
> ment.

It is evident that Madame played a vital part in the preliminary
secret negotiations before the Treaty of Dover, but she incurred
the displeasure of King Louis for seeming to favour her
brother's interests during the summer (1669).

At the beginning of July Lord Arundell returned to England
bearing a personal letter from Louis to Charles, and the answers
to the King of England's proposals. It is clear that the Abbé

Montagu, Queen Henrietta Maria's almoner, a fervent Roman Catholic, who wanted England to be reconciled to that Church, translated the English papers into French for Louis and Madame.

Louis considered that Charles should postpone declaring himself a Roman Catholic until he was convinced that he was strong enough to do so, for he was aware that most people in England were opposed to Roman Catholicism. Louis wanted a concerted attack by France and Britain on Holland. The most sensitive part of the negotiations was the naval expansion of France. Charles was eager that Louis should promise to build no more ships, but the King of France objected to this at first merely contenting himself with a vague promise that he would do nothing to rouse English jealousy of his maritime power.[10] Under pressure from Arundell, Louis promised to cease ship-building for a year.[11] It is clear that some extremely hard bargaining was adopted by both countries in the preliminary negotiations. It was a clever move on Charles's part to release Louis from his undertaking to cease building ships for one year, for he thought that the King of France's candour and generosity were the best security. Provided Louis allowed him £200,000 for the purpose of supplying the needs of his army and naval forces, Charles was prepared to join the proposed concerted attack on Holland. He was willing to do so before he made his declaration of Catholicity.

It is fascinating to conjecture whether or not Charles ever seriously intended to make his declaration either before the Dutch war or subsequently. Both Madame and Louis were convinced that Charles was in earnest.[12] If Charles was insincere regarding his religious protestations, it seems curious that he was able to deceive even his 'deare, deare sister' herself a devoted Catholic. Did not the Abbé Bossuet say in his *Oraison Funèbre*[13] after her death 'who could sufficiently express her ardour for the restoration of this faith in the kingdom of England?' Louis, too, had much affection for Madame and referred to her in his letter to Charles at the end of August as 'the intermediary of this negotiation, as she is herself so natural a bond of union between us'.

It is with a sense of sadness that one reads Charles's last known letter to his sister in the green volume among the Quai D'Orsay archives, referring to Arundell's possible scruples concerning the negotiations and Charles's certainty that Arlington was loyal to him. 'I shall write to you tomorrow by L'Abbe Pregnany ... and in truth I am just now going to a new play that I have much commended and so I am yours C.R.' He ends on a characteristic light note.

Towards the end of August Madame gave birth to her younger daughter, who was to be christened Anne Marie, and to be known as Mademoiselle de Valois. It is surprising that Henriette could turn her mind to vital diplomatic negotiations when her private life with Monsieur was daily becoming more wretched. She was scarcely mistress in her own household. The Chevalier de Lorraine ruled Monsieur, and his insolence was intolerable. Madame passed the summer (1669) at St. Cloud, and it was there while she was recovering from the birth of her child that she heard of the death of her beloved mother at Colombes. Père Cyprien records that her conversation until the end retained its gaiety and wit. M. Yvelin and M. Esprit, Monsieur and Madame's physicians consulted with Monsieur Vallot, King Louis's physician and Monsieur Duquesne. Henriette Maria suffered from insomnia and pains in her side. Vallot prescribed a grain of opium to be added to the medicines already given her. The Queen at first objected to this, saying: 'An astrologer told me, years ago, in England, a grain would be the cause of my death, and I fear M. Vallot's grain may be that fatal grain.' Besides, she added: 'Mayerne always warned me against taking any such drug.'[14] However, she took the opium pills on the night of 9 September and never woke again.

Monsieur, behaved most objectionably, for he claimed all his mother-in-law's property under French law for his wife, declaring that she was the only one of her children living in France.

Madame did not approve of her husband's action and tactfully said that she would prefer to await her brother's pleasure in the matter. Since Queen Henrietta Maria had made no will, under English law Charles was her sole heir. Many valuable pictures, including Titians and Van Dykes formerly belonging to Charles I, were removed to England. Yet Charles II was very generous to his sister, giving her the country house at Colombes and most of the furniture. She was delighted when Ralph Montagu presented her with some very valuable pearls, which she had often worn during her mother's lifetime.

Deeply grieved by her death, Madame remained at St. Cloud, while Monsieur to her relief left for Chambord during September to join the King and Queen.

Madame de La Fayette frequently visited her, and it was now that she decided to continue the writing of the *Mémoires* that had been temporarily abandoned during 1665, thinking that it might help to soften the shock of Queen Henrietta Maria's death for her beloved friend. Madame took a childish delight in these *Mémoires*, insisting on reading over what Madame de La Fayette had written, the day before, and sometimes making various corrections in her own hand.

It was now that Madame's friendship with the Abbé Bossuet became more intimate. He would often visit her at St. Cloud to discuss religious matters. Madame de La Fayette was also an intimate friend of the great preacher's and wrote of him: 'He is the most honest and straightforward of men, the gentlest and the frankest speaker who has been known at Court.' He had been born at Dijon in 1627, the son of bourgeois parents, and he was appointed Bishop of Condom in 1669.[15] He was immensely learned, gentle and compassionate, and deeply esteemed by King Louis, who did not disgrace Bossuet when he dared to reproach the King for his private conduct. What he really excelled at was the *Oraison Funèbre* or obituary sermon, for he was an artist in his delicate choice of the French language. He is superb when contrasting the impermanence of earthly glory with the eternity of the spirit. Monsieur and Madame were both later present on 16 November 1669 at the Church of St. Marie in Chaillot when Bossuet preached the *Oraison Funèbre* of Queen Henrietta Maria.

Lord Arlington had sent Madame a letter in which he had expressed his sympathy that her baby was a daughter, and the hope that she would might yet have a son, for she had longed for one ever since the Duc de Valois's early death. Arlington could not resist writing that his old enemy, Lord Clarendon now in exile in France, was responsible for a temporary coldness between King Louis and Madame. She herself did not think so, for she was aware that Louis resented her putting her brother's interests before his own. She had tried to warn her brother of her suspicions by sending him a message by a Page of the Backstairs, possibly Elloaies[16]* (as mentioned in Charles's letter of 6 June). The real truth is that Henrietta never forgot that she was an English Princess. Her brother mattered to her more than anybody else. Enclosed in her letter to Lord Arlington is one for her brother. It is certainly the most important letter she ever wrote to Charles, revealing as it does that she had a very astute brain, and that she was very gifted. There can be no doubt of her vital role in bringing about the alliance between Charles and Louis. It is a fallacy, however, to suppose that she was acting entirely in the French interest. How cleverly she puts to Charles the advantages of 'entering into a league with Louis against Holland'. A trained diplomat with many years of experience could not have argued the case more forcefully or with more ability than the Princess, who was only twenty-five. She reminds Charles that he had need of France to ensure the success of the design about R. (Religion), and there is very little likelihood of your obtaining what you desire from the King except on condition that you enter into a league with him against Holland.... Indeed what is there more glorious and more profitable than to extend the confines of your kingdom beyond the sea and to become supreme in commerce, which is what your people most passionately desire and what

* Clifford Mss. This letter in the original French is at Ugbrooke Park.

will probably never occur so long as the Republic of Holland exists...'[17]

Charles throughout his life showed little sympathy for Anglicanism, but he constantly baffled his Protestant subjects as to his real religious beliefs. He was realistic enough to understand the political importance of adhering to Anglicanism, although he privately thought that Catholicism was the proper religion for gentlemen. Did he not owe his life to some extent to the loyal Roman Catholics or recusants* who had sheltered him after Worcester? There is abundant evidence to show that he was at heart in sympathy with the Church of Rome. Cardinal de Retz believed that he favoured that church during his exile. It might be correct to describe Charles as a secret church-papist.[18]

Madame was opposed to Charles confiding the design to Pope Clement IX since his health was very feeble and he might not live long. She considered that his successor whoever that might be would provide every facility when her brother were to make a public declaration that he was a Roman Catholic, so that his pontificate might be honoured by the reconciliation of England to the Church of Rome.

On 3 October Lord Arundell returned to France to inform King Louis that King Charles favoured the Treaty being negotiated in England since the continued presence of an English envoy in France would arouse suspicions. There can be no doubt that Madame played a vital part at this stage of the negotiations. Arundell was instructed by King Charles to show her all the papers. He had to warn her of the need for the greatest secrecy. Above all, Colbert de Croissy in London must not let anybody else see the papers concerning the negotiations and do all the deciphering and writing of the despatches himself.[19] After the documents had been translated into French by the Abbé Montagu, Arundell was told to consult Madame about the best means of seeking an interview with King Louis. He was to explain to the King of France his reasons for wanting

* The recusants refused to attend the public worship of the Church of England.

the actual treaty signed in England. It was his delicate duty to attempt to reassure Louis as to Charles's attitude towards the Triple Alliance. Now for the first time Charles had agreed that Colbert de Croissy should be admitted into the secret and negotiate the treaty on behalf of Louis.[20] The King of France had always wanted his ambassador to be entrusted with the secret.

It would seem that Sir Thomas Clifford's part in composing the original drafts of the Treaty of Dover was of great importance. Many of the papers are in his handwriting. These were shown the Secretary of State, Lord Arlington and King Charles for further consideration.

These preliminary projects for a Treaty were discussed by the King, Arlington, Clifford, Arundell, and Bellings at a meeting in the lodgings of Father Patrick Maginn, a Roman Catholic priest, who had no knowledge of the purpose of the meeting. Father Patrick had occasionally carried Charles's letters to Minette in France. Charles had written to her on 22 March: 'I desire you to be kinde to the poore man, for he is as honest a man as lives, and pray derect your phesisian to have a care of him.' Since the French Ambassador was present, the discussion was conducted in French, but Clifford's knowledge of the language was so rudimentary that Charles acted as interpreter for him. Colbert de Croissy was much concerned that the English commissioners were making outrageous demands, and it was indeed only after many months and after a good deal of friction, that agreement was reached; at one point he even thought that the negotiations might collapse. Charles II, the Duke of York and Arlington insisted that the Principal command of conduct of the naval operations must be left in British hands.

XIII

Madame's Domestic Troubles

The autumn and winter of 1669–70 was a very unhappy period in the life of Madame. Her marriage with Monsieur had almost reached an open rupture. Philippe was as infatuated as ever with the Chevalier de Lorraine, and the Chevalier treated Madame with intolerable insolence.

Henriette missed the wise counsel of Cosnac, though she kept closely in touch with the Bishop by means of a secret correspondence through Madame de St. Chaumont, one of her closest friends and governess of her children. He still languished in exile and Henriette implored King Louis to have him recalled, but Louis remained obdurate, having been told by Louvois that the Bishop was a dangerous character. Henriette blamed herself that Cosnac's misfortunes were mainly owing to his attachment to her interests. To compensate him for his unjust treatment, together with Madame de St. Chaumont she thought of an ingenious idea. Since her brother's longed for conversion would give him marked influence with the Pope, she would avail herself of it and obtain for the Bishop of Valence a Cardinal's hat. She wrote to Cosnac on 10 June:

> This idea may, I understand, well appear visionary to you at first, since the authorities on whom these favours depend, seemed so little inclined to show you any good. But to explain this enigma you must know that among an infinite number of affairs, which are now in course of arrangement between France and England, the last-named country is likely before long, to become of such importance in the eyes of Rome, and there will be so great a readiness to oblige the King my brother

in whatever he may wish, that I am quite certain nothing that he asks will be refused. I have already begged him without mentioning names, to ask for a Cardinal's hat and he has promised me. . . .[1]

Cosnac did not take the suggestion very seriously, though grateful to Madame for her kindness and thoughtfulness. Madame was hurt, and referred to the matter again in her correspondence with him. The Princess's eagerness for her brother's ultimate conversion to Roman Catholicism blinded her as to the hostile state of feeling against that religion in England.

Madame continually wrote to Cosnac of her esteem for him. She confided in him about her domestic troubles.

Not a day passes, [she told him] that good Père Zoccoli [Monsieur's confessor] begs me to be kind to the Chevalier de Lorraine. . . . . I assure him that, in order to like a man who is the cause of all my sorrows past and present it would be necessary for me to have some esteem for him, or else owe him some debt of gratitude, both of which are absolutely impossible, after he has behaved so badly[2]

Cosnac still retained the compromising letters from Lorraine, which had been found in the casket of Mademoiselle de Fiennes. During October she wrote asking him to send or bring them to her. Cosnac knew that he was watched by Louvois, and that King Louis had ordered him to remain away from Paris. Nevertheless, he rashly decided to travel to St. Denis where he had secretly arranged to meet Madame. It was a journey fraught with danger, for Louvois's spies watched his every movement. Making for Paris, and in disguise, he unfortunately fell ill in some lodgings near the Rue St. Denis. Fearful that Lorraine's compromising letters would fall into the hands of his enemies, the Bishop sent his nephew Claude de Cosnac de La Marque, who was with him in Paris, with the letters, charging him to see that they were handed to Madame de St. Chaumont, who could give them to Madame. There was a knock on the door, and a police officer named Desgrez followed by numerous police-spies entered. They arrested Cosnac on the grounds that he was a notorious forger, although probably aware of his real identity. Cosnac was too frank a man to make a successful secret agent. Taking his pectoral cross from under his pillow, he announced that he was Bishop of Valence. Cosnac now realized that he had been betrayed by the physician he had consulted. Unfortunately the Bishop had overlooked one short note from Madame de St. Chaumont, and this was taken to Louvois and handed to King Louis. Poor Cosnac was taken in his dressing-gown to the prison of For-L'Évêque where he was treated as a common prisoner and then forced to endure further exile in L'Ile Jourdain near Toulouse.

Francis Vernon, a Secretary at the English Embassy relates that Monsieur himself informed his wife that the Bishop of Valence had been arrested, and Madame flew into a passion. The seizure of Madame de St. Chaumont's letter gave King Louis an excuse to involve the governess in Cosnac's disgrace. For some time he had been prejudiced against this lady by Madame de Montespan, her inveterate enemy.

According to Ralph Montagu's account sent to Lord Arlington, King Louis ordered the Maréchal de Turenne to bear a message to Madame that she must dismiss Madame de St. Chaumont from her employment. Henriette asked Montagu to argue the case, with the King, but it availed nothing. 'Madame desires', he wrote, 'that the King (Charles II) would take no notice of it to the French Ambassador further than thus to tell him that he hears King Louis has used his sister lately very unkindly.' Louis told his brother that he believed Madame would complain to King Charles, who was tactless enough to repeat this to his wife. He was a terrible chatterbox. Louis said, 'Well, let her be whose sister she will, she will obey me.'[3] All the same such an act would harm relations with England at a time when Louis was ardently seeking an alliance. Ralph Montagu thought that King Louis's chief pleasure was 'to domineer and insult those that are in his power'. He thanked God that Arlington and he served so good a master, hoping no doubt that the Secretary of State would show King Charles his letter.

Montagu's advice to Charles was very judicious. He wrote on 12 December:

> The King here (Louis) is sufficiently convinced of all the impertinences and insolencies of the Chevalier de Lorraine and doth at this time both desire and stand in need so much of your friendship that I believe in a little time that he may be brought to remove him from about Monsieur, if he sees it is a thing your Majesty really insists upon.

Montagu was aware that Charles was longing to see his sister and suggested that the King should write her to visit him in England during the following spring.

> I assure you, Sire, not only all the French but the Dutch, the Swedish and the Spanish ministers are in expectation of what your Majesty will do in this business, for they all know Madame is the thing in the world that is dearest to you.

Charles vented his anger against the disgraceful treatment given his sister by his vigorous complaints to Colbert de Croissy. The ambassador's attempt to justify Louis's action in dismissing Madame de St. Chaumont was hardly convincing, nor was his assurance that it was not intended in any way as an insult.[4] Arlington told Colbert de Croissy that Madame's participation in the grandè affaire was so essential that she must be conciliated. Louis always liked to have news of Charles II's ladies and his ambassador wrote on 6 January 1670 to tell him 'Madame de Castlemen was yesterday in great danger of dying'. Actually she lived for many years, although she had now lost her influence.

Much to Madame's annoyance, Monsieur had his way in appointing the Maréchale de Clérembault as governess to his children, though his wife would have preferred her friend Madame de La Fayette.

The Chevalier de Lorraine now boasted that he had been

responsible for ruining Madame's friends. He even spread abroad reports that a divorce was impending between Monsieur and Madame. It so happened, however, that the Bishop of Langres, a favourite of Gaston, the late Duke of Orléans, had just died, and the revenues of two abbeys became vacant. They formed part of the appanage of the Dukes of Orléans, and Monsieur was free to dispose of them as he wished subject to the consent of the King. He immediately went to see King Louis, who waꞌ on his way to Versailles, to beg his brother to give Lorraine the revenues of the two abbeys, to be met with an absolute refusal. Louis told Philippe that the Chevalier was not a fit person to be given Church benefices. Monsieur lost his temper, and vowed that he never wished to see his brother's face again. He then repeated to Lorraine what the King had said. The Chevalier made some extremely offensive comments about King Louis, and somebody lost no time in reporting what Lorraine had said to the King. When Monsieur learnt that Louis had ordered his favourite's arrest, he fainted. Monsieur was present when Le Comte d'Ayen arrested the Chevalier, and he had to surrender his sword.[5] He was imprisoned in Pierre Encise near Paris.

Monsieur was very nasty to his wife, blaming her for his favourite's disgrace. Actually she had done little to bring it about, although she had certainly wished him far removed from her husband. Madame was now on better terms with La Grande Mademoiselle and confided in her: 'I have no reason to like the Chevalier de Lorraine because we have not got on well together.' However, strange as it may seem, Henriette was genuinely distressed at Monsieur's pain caused by the Chevalier's arrest.[6] La Grande Mademoiselle was shocked by Monsieur's unkindness to his wife in Paris, although Madame spoke gently to her husband. According to Montagu's account of this affair sent to Arlington (1 February), Madame tried to intercede between the King and his brother. 'The King declared that he loved his brother so well that he was resolved to remove anybody that could do ill offices between them.'[7] Montagu reported that Monsieur had carried off his wife to Villers-Cotterets, a rather desolate place in the depths of winter. Monsieur was so incensed when Louis ordered his favourite's removal to the Château d'if, near Marseilles, an impregnable island-fortress, that he refused to sleep with his wife. This caused further scandal. When Ralph Montagu was granted an interview with King Louis a few days later he took the opportunity of recommending him to treat her 'kindly as the person in the world that was the dearest to the King my master'. Louis told Montagu that it was not he who was angry with Monsieur, but his brother with him. If he stayed away too long from Court, he might lose the natural tenderness he always had for him. When one studies Ralph Montagu's letters among the French papers in the Public Record Office, one is impressed by the young diplomat's subtlety, and ability. If he was later unscrupulous about obtaining money, he knew how to spend it. Montagu was a man of magnificent tastes, and he was to build Boughton House in Northamptonshire, inspired by Versailles and Montagu House in Bloomsbury.* Montagu was not yet initiated into all the secrets of King Charles's foreign policy. It was from Madame that he first learnt that her brother intended to make a secret alliance with King Louis against the Dutch.

In the solitude of Villers-Cotterets Madame poured out her heart in touching letters to Madame de St. Chaumont. Later she was to write to her on 26 March from St. Germain:

I see from the ashes of Monsieur's love for the Chevalier, as from the dragon's teeth, a whole brood of fresh favourites are likely to spring up to vex me. Monsieur now puts his trust in the little Marsan [another prince of the house of Lorraine] and the Chevalier de Beuvron, not to speak of the false face of the Marquis de Villeroy, who prides himself on being his

---

* The first Montagu House was burnt down in 1686. Ralph Montagu built a house to replace it later purchased by the Government to become the British Museum.

friend, and only seeks his own interests, regardless of those of Monsieur, or of the Chevalier.[8]

Meanwhile from Villers-Cotterets, Monsieur wrote to Colbert, the King's chief minister, who possessed some influence with him. He visited him and tried hard to persuade him to return to Court, but Monsieur obstinately repeated that he would never return unless the Chevalier was recalled.

Distressed by her husband's wholly unreasonable behaviour, it was a relief to Madame to turn her mind to the negotiations in the Secret Treaty. Towards the end of January 1670 she received a vital document in Sir Thomas Clifford's handwriting, summarising England's attitude towards the naval war.[9] The British point of view was that if King Charles was to consent to a war against Holland, it was a mistake to suppose that 30 or 40 English ships joining with the French fleet could prosecute the war with advantage and security to England. It was essential for the King of England to have sufficient supplies to set out his whole naval force. In his insistence on English naval supremacy Charles was fully backed by the Duke of York, by Lord Arlington and especially by Sir Thomas Clifford, who, mindful of his experiences at sea during the Dutch war, realized like his master, that England could only be great by sea. The Duke of York stoutly maintained that in naval matters the English must have the superiority over the French, and that the combined fleet must be commanded by an Englishman.

The question of a subsidy for King Charles also caused considerable consternation among the French negotiators, for Charles at first demanded 10,000,000 livres for the war against Holland.[10] Louis acted reasonably in telling Colbert de Croissy that he was amazed at the extravagance of the proposals. Madame had been deeply shocked. Colbert de Croissy told Charles that he must reduce his financial demands, if the negotiations were to continue.

Throughout the winter 1669–70, Charles again and again expressed his longing to see his sister to Colbert de Croissy.

Louis was eager, too, that his sister-in-law should visit Charles, but was well aware that Monsieur would be uncooperative and indeed try to prevent his wife making the journey. Louis proposed during the following spring that the French Court should travel to Flanders to view the new province ceded to France by Spain by the Treaty of Aix-la-Chapelle. It would also be a favourable opportunity for Madame to sail from Dunkirk to visit her brother in England. It would hardly arouse the suspicions of the Dutch.

Thomas Belasye Lord Fauconberg* a son-in-law of Oliver Cromwell was about to leave for Italy in February, having been appointed Ambassador to Venice, Florence and Savoy. He arrived in St. Germain bearing an official request that Madame should be allowed to visit England that spring. He now heard about King Louis's quarrel with his brother, and of Monsieur's withdrawal from Court. He wrote Arlington:

> I sent Mr Dodington [his secretary] to Villers-Cotterets to waite upon Madame, ... but that I held it improper to attend her Highnesse there with the letters untill I had first given her knowledge of it, not being assured how Monsieur might receive me, in regard I had none for him ...[11]

It is evident that John Dodington was enchanted by Madame's gracious manner. He wrote home:

> Madame received me with all imaginable kindness much beyond which a man of my figure could pretend to and did me the favour to give me a full howers private discourse with her, and perceiving that I was not unacquainted with her affaires ... she was pleased to tell me she had designed to see the King her brother at Dover as this Court passes by Calais to Flanders....

Dodington wrote that Madame was adored by everybody 'and hath more spirit than ever her mother had' ... 'The King of

---

* He married Cromwell's daughter Mary. Formerly a strong adherent of Cromwell.

France is extraordinary kind to Madame.' She told Dodington that she and King Louis had agreed that King Charles, the Duke of York, and Lord St. Albans should write letters to Monsieur requesting that she might be allowed to visit her brother at Dover when the French Court departed on its journey to Flanders.[12]

Fortunately Monsieur was by this time extremely tired of Villers-Cotterets in the depths of winter, and longed to return to the gaieties of Court. It did not require much persuasion on the part of Colbert who visited Monsieur on 22 February, to induce Monsieur to return to St. Germain. Lorraine was now a prisoner on parole at Marseilles, and Monsieur showered him with loving letters.

Madame's part in the secret negotiations was absolutely vital, and Louis wanted to consult her in St. Germain. Dodington and Vernon the secretary at the British Embassy reported that Louis was very generous to Madame, charging Colbert to give jewels, gloves, perfumes, and money. Dodington wrote that the King presented her with many rich curiosities, and that she had 'a great influence on this prince'. Madame was much beloved at the French Court, and there was general rejoicing when she returned to Court. As Madame de Suze expressed it: 'Since Madame left us, joy is no longer to be seen at St. Germain.' When Fauconberg visited her, she impressed him as 'a princess of extraordinary address and conduct'.

Everybody, however, noticed how ill and pale Madame looked. Her expression was sad, reminding us of the Lely portrait in the Guildhall at Exeter, painted shortly before her death.

Mademoiselle, who had been jealous of Madame, now cherished kindly sentiments for her. She thought that Monsieur's treatment of his wife was outrageous. One day Madame said affectionately to her: 'We have never been so intimate, my cousin as we ought to be, but you, I know, have a good heart. Mine is not a bad one. Let us be friends.' Few people could resist Henrietta's charm. When her little daughter was christened Anne Marie in the Chapel of the Palais-Royal, Mademoiselle was godmother.

At St. Germain, Madame and her husband occupied their usual apartments in the Château Neuf, but according to La Grande Mademoiselle, Louis put at his sister-in-law's disposal in the old palace a room near the King's apartments where they could work together during the afternoon.

Monsieur was abnormally jealous, resentful that his brother showed such esteem and affection for his wife, and of her prestige at Court. Unfortunately he now learnt from the mischievous Chevalier de Lorraine with whom he corresponded every day, of Madame's proposed visit to England. Louis was astounded when his brother told him that he already knew of it. It transpired that Maréchal de Turenne who was in the secret, had been indiscreet enough to mention it to one of Madame's ladies, Madame de Côetquen. The gallant elderly warrior greatly admired this lady, but she was infatuated with Lorraine and concealed nothing from him in her letters. Lorraine at once told Monsieur. Turenne was much embarrassed when Louis taxed him with it, and had to admit the truth. He ruefully said to the King that of course he had not mentioned Louis's designs on Holland. Turenne's indiscretion amused the King, but he warned him not to confide anymore secrets to Madame de Côetquen. When her mistress gently reproached her, her lady-in-waiting fell on her knees, imploring her forgiveness, for she was ardently in love with Lorraine. Louis found Philippe more obstinate than ever. In one of his towering rages he informed his brother, far from allowing his wife to visit England, he would not even give his permission for her to go to Flanders. Monsieur's grudging attitude was keenly resented by King Charles, as Colbert de Croissy reported to Louis. It was his brother Jean Baptiste Colbert, who managed to persuade Monsieur to agree that Madame should make a short visit to Dover, provided he accompanied her. Ralph Montagu wrote that Colbert had more power with Monsieur than anybody.

He could not bear the thought that she should get all the glory for the Treaty. As Monsieur was a gossip one wonders how the matter remained a great secret.

It was imperative that Monsieur should be prevented from accompanying his wife to England, particularly because he had not been apprized of the negotiations up to this point. It was Charles who invented a reasonable excuse. He maintained that it would be unseemly for Monsieur to visit him unless at the same time his brother the Duke of York were to travel to Calais to see the King of France. Unfortunately the Duke of York could not do so.

Charles was most anxious to invite his sister to London, but Monsieur would not hear of it. Dover was then a mere village with few facilities and it would be difficult to entertain his sister there. Colbert de Croissy wrote to Lionne to inform him that King Charles was sending Sidney Godolphin to represent to Monsieur the objections to Dover. Not only the poor accommodation, but the air was very bad there. These considerations would prevent Queen Catherine and the Duchess of York from going there.[13] Louis was tired of his brother's sulkiness and now peremptorily told him that for the good of the state Madame must go to England. With the greatest reluctance, Monsieur at last consented to it, but stipulated that Madame must not remain with her brother more than three days, and that she could not go further than Dover. He also tried to stipulate that the Duke of Monmouth should be sent to Holland, while Madame was in England.[14] Monsieur hoped that the Chevalier would be recalled to France, but Louis merely gave his permission for Lorraine to go to Italy where he was now free.

While Montagu reported in late March that Madame and her husband were on the worst possible terms, the Marquis de St. Maurice wrote to the Duke of Savoy that Monsieur was sleeping with his wife every day in a last attempt to frustrate the journey, were she to become pregnant. The marriage in any case was almost on the rocks.

Louis treated Madame most generously, giving her 200,000

crowns towards the expenses of her proposed journey. He himself took considerable care in selecting her suite. Madame was delighted that her close friends the Comte and Comtesse de Gramont (the former Elizabeth Hamilton) were to accompany her. There was great competition among the Princess's ladies for the honour of being included in her suite. William Perwich a Secretary at the British Embassy, however, reported that 'the Duchess of Elboeuf and many ladies of that quality begin to scruple going with Madam to Dover, doubting about the Tabouret'. What mattered in France was the jealous observance of marks of distinction, of the rights of birth. Sièges pliantes (folding chairs) must be given to princesses, and tabourets (stools) to the ladies.[15] Perwich wrote of the excitement before the journey 'the preparations of gold embroideries for saille clothes'. He wrote:

> Some ruffians wanting money on Wednesday last went to one of the secretaires de Rey and being private with him told him their necessities wch he must supply with a thousand pistills, but the poor gent. endeavouring to cry out for help was stab'd and I think dead by this time, two of them are taken.

When Monsieur learnt that Philippe de Lorraine had become the confidant and probable lover of Marie Mancini, the Princess Colonna in Rome, it is difficult to gauge his feelings, for she was a childhood friend. She had once loved his brother.

During that winter and spring, Princess Henriette was frequently visited by the Abbé Bossuet, who had just been appointed Bishop of Condom. Disillusioned and sad, she turned more and more to the consolations of religion. On one occasion she said to him with her customary *douceur*: 'I am afraid I have thought too little of my soul. If it is not too late, help me to find the way of salvation.' To show her friendship for the eloquent preacher, she ordered her jeweller to make an emerald ring to be presented to him.

163

XIV

Secret Diplomacy at Dover

On 28 April 1670 the Court set out for Flanders. The pretext of visiting the towns recently annexed by France concealed the real object of the journey, the proposed visit of Madame to Dover. In the great State-coach rode King Louis and his Queen Marie-Thérèse, together with Madame and Madame de Montespan now triumphant over her rival the Duchesse de La Vallière. To Madame de Sévigné, the King and Queen were the Fire and the Snow while Montespan was the Torrent and La Vallière the Dew. In the next coach came Mademoiselle and the Dauphin. The cavalry was commanded by the fiery Comte de Lauzun 'One of the smallest men that God ever made,' as described by Bussy-Rabatin. Mademoiselle was in love with him. Their coach was followed by carriages containing the nobility and attendants in charge of the furniture, tapestries, and gold and silver plate, all designed to impress the people in the towns through which the royal party passed with the atavistic image of kingship. Before and behind marched an army of 30,000 men.

Unfortunately not even Le Roi Soleil could command the weather. Most of the time it was atrocious; torrential rain fell incessantly, making the roads impassable and causing the carriages to get stuck in the mud.

Madame usually so gay and lively, felt ill, and seemed to those around her very despondent. According to Mademoiselle,[1] Henriette hardly touched her food, contenting herself with a little milk. She suffered in spirit, though she never complained and retired to rest for the night whenever possible. Monsieur had insisted on his various treasures being transported on this journey

164

and was not much upset until he discovered that his cosmetics had been lost.

When he joined Madame in her coach he was very disagreeable to her, saying in front of the Queen and La Grande Mademoiselle that an astrologer had recently predicted that he would have several wives. Then glancing at his wife he added: 'Evidently Madame will not live long, so the prediction seems likely to be fulfilled.' The royal ladies were horrified at Monsieur's callous behaviour, though Madame was so inured to it she was almost indifferent.

When the royal travellers approached Landrecies, they were much dismayed to discover that the Sambre had overflowed its banks and that the only bridge had collapsed. They had not eaten or drunk anything for several hours, and the King said that it was necessary to spend the night in a wretched two-roomed farmhouse that lay nearby. Queen Marie-Thérèse behaved like a petulant child, complaining that she was hungry and that she would be ill if she could not sleep. The King, however, did not lose his good humour. He tried to reassure his wife. Mattresses were spread on the floor of the farmhouse by the attendants. 'How horrible!' she cried in her stupid way. 'What? All of us sleep together?' Louis merely said: 'Where is the harm in lying on mattresses fully dressed? Ask my cousin what she thinks and let us follow her advice.' Mademoiselle supported the King. Marie-Thérèse refused to touch the soup when it was brought, and it was thin and tasteless, but the King, Monsieur, Madame and Mademoiselle were so famished that they ate it all up. Madame was almost in a state of collapse, but she made light of the discomfort, thinking it an adventure. The chicken was so tough that the royal travellers took its legs and had difficulty in tearing it apart.

The Queen lay down on the mattress nearest the fire, near her two ladies Madame de Thianges and Madame de Bethune, then on separate mattresses almost touching one another. Monsieur, Madame, King Louis, Mademoiselle, the Duchesse de La Vallière next her rival Madame de Montespan and other ladies. They had all put on dressing-gowns over their clothes and night-caps. Madame de Thianges relieved the tension when she humorously said that she heard cattle and donkeys in the adjoining stable, reminding her of the birth of Our Lord. Even the Queen laughed at this.

Monsieur de Louvois brought news at 4 a.m. that the bridge had been repaired. It was a strange spectacle that ghostly morning when the ladies pale without their rouge and stifling their yawns through lack of sleep prepared for their departure.

Madame was relieved that her husband only rarely joined her in the coach as they rode through Flanders, for he preferred instead to ride through the towns at the head of his regiment. At Courtrai, she looked radiant when she was greeted by English envoys, who told her that King Charles was already in Dover and that Lord Sandwich was awaiting her orders with the English fleet. The King and Monsieur accompanied Madame as far as Lille where she was to leave for Dunkirk. William Perwich, who was at Lille, wrote to Sir Joseph Williamson that magnificent preparations were being made for the King's arrival, 'bonfires, fireworks and fountains to run with wine'.[2] When Ralph Montagu, the English ambassador arrived, he was offered a rousing reception. 'My Lord Douglas as the head of his Regiment made him a compliment of vollys and great guns from the Ramparts.' The Douglas was the Scots regiment in the service of Louis XIV, precursor of the Royal Scots.

Mademoiselle relates in her *Mémoires* that Monsieur spoke with so much anger against his wife that she realised there was no chance of a reconciliation.

While Madame was at Lille, she was visited by the able French ambassador at the Hague Monsieur de Pomponne, and he was impressed, like everybody, by her grace and capacity for business. She complained of Sir William Temple, the diplomatist, a great friend of Holland, who she considered was hostile to France. Colbert de Croissy, who arrived from England, told Louis that there were rumours that King Charles

II would divorce Queen Catherine because she could not have children. The rumours proved unfounded.

Louis was anxious that his sister-in-law should receive every honour and a suite of no less than 237 persons attended her on her journey to Dover. Charles, however, had expressed a wish that she should come with a small suite, for there was very limited accommodation in Dover. The most important members were the Marechal du Plessis, the Bishop of Tournay and as already mentioned the Comte and Comtesse de Gramont were of the party. Among Henriette's five maids-of-honour was Louise de Keroualle, the daughter of an impoverished Breton nobleman: '*une délicieuse poupée*', with her baby, pretty face as she has been described.[3] It was during the evening of 24 May (new calendar) that Madame and her suite embarked in the English ships at Dunkirk for Dover. At 5 o'clock the following morning she was up on deck eager to catch the first glimpses of the Cliffs of Dover when she descried a boat being rowed at full speed towards the fleet. It was King Charles together with the Duke of York, the Duke of Monmouth and her Cousin Prince Rupert, son of the winter queen Elizabeth of Bohemia. There was a radiant look on Minette's face as she embraced Charles, and as she set foot once again on English soil she must have recalled her visit to England during the late autumn and winter (1660–1) when Father Cyprien de Gamaches had accompanied her mother and herself to Dover. Then she had been an inexperienced princess, now she was feted and loved by everybody.

She was conducted to her quarters in the mediaeval castle standing so proudly and resplendently on the hill overlooking the harbour and the village as she saw it that summer day. Dover Castle, to a great extent the work of the Plantagenet King Henry II was already almost five hundred years old in 1670. The Chapel of St. Thomas particularly pleased her. In 1216 the Castle had been besieged by the Dauphin Louis of France, invited by King John's rebellious barons to accept the English Crown, but it had been stoutly defended by Hubert de Burgh.

'Madame is here in perfect health,' wrote Colbert de Croissy to his Foreign Minister Lionne. So she may have appeared to him, but the truth was otherwise. The journey to Flanders had imposed a severe strain on her delicate health. However, her gaiety, her sparkle, her obvious pleasure in the companionship of Charles and of his son Monmouth, and the beautiful early summer sunshine, such a contrast to the atrocious weather in Flanders, created a contrary impression.

Charles lost no time in getting down to business with Madame, Arlington, Clifford, and the others. Colbert de Croissy wrote to Louis that Madame had told him that she had shaken her brother's resolution and that he was now disposed to declare war on Holland immediately.[4] Actually Charles's mind had almost certainly been made up already, and it is very doubtful whether his sister influenced him. Madame, however, suggested that now an immediate war had been determined, Turenne should come over to England at once to discuss military measures. Charles, too, thought it an excellent idea. Colbert de Croissy demurred at it, arguing that the presence of France's Commander-in-Chief in England could not fail to arouse suspicions in Holland. Madame's tact and charm were invaluable in removing the obstacles which still delayed the conclusion of the commercial Treaty. Both Charles and Minette agreed that it would be advisable to postpone any public acknowledgement of the King's change of religion. Again there is the fatal doubt whether Charles ever seriously intended it, fully aware as he was of the anti-Catholic sentiments of the majority of his subjects and of the danger of losing his throne.

Madame was overjoyed when Louis wrote from Dunkirk on 31 May, saying that Madame might prolong her stay for another ten or twelve days, since the original three days granted by Monsieur were not sufficient to complete the negotiations. He had obtained Monsieur's permission for this purpose.

To make her stay as agreeable as possible, Charles now arranged that Queen Catherine and the Duchess of York should come to Dover from London. It is the first time that Madame had met Charles's Portuguese-born queen, and they were immediately on excellent terms. She later told Mademoiselle that although the Queen was not beautiful, she was a good woman and so frank and amiable that you could not help liking her. Madame was already acquainted with her other sister-in-law, the former Anne Hyde and she would be able to give her news of her daughter Anne, who had been having treatment for her poor eyesight in France. Among the Queen's ladies was 'La Belle Stuart', Minette's early friend in France.

Among those at Dover was the Duke of Buckingham, who had once followed his Princess back to France from Portsmouth. Madame whilst cleverly concealing the contents of the secret Treaty from him, took the opportunity of reconciling the two rivals Buckingham and Arlington. She preferred Clifford to Arlington, for she was to write later to Clifford that 'he was less hard to please'.

On 1 June the Secret Treaty was signed at Dover by Colbert de Croissy on behalf of France, and by Lord Arlington, Lord Arundel, Sir Thomas Clifford, and Sir Richard Bellings for England. Sir Richard was a Roman Catholic, and the best French scholar in England. One of the two original copies of the Secret Treaty* written in French by Bellings was entrusted to Sir Thomas Clifford and is today among Lord Clifford's Mss. at Ugbrooke Park, Devon.

The framework of the Treaty owed much to the arduous work of Arlington, Clifford, and Colbert de Croissy acting on instructions from Lionne and King Louis.

It has been summarised by Cyril Hughes Hartmann, so it is unnecessary to discuss it in detail.

The King of England, being convinced of the truth of the Catholic religion and resolved to make a public declaration of it and to reconcile himself with the Roman Church as soon as he was able, was to receive from the King of France the sum of 2,000,000 livres tournois (about £160,000), half to be paid

* The other copy is now in the Dépôt des Traites at the Quai D'Orsay.

three months after the exchange of ratifications and half three months later, to aid him in making this declaration. King Louis also promised, if need be, to assist the King of England with 6000 troops. One important point was that the time of Charles's declaration was to be left entirely to his own discretion. It was only on his deathbed during February 1685 that Charles acknowledged that he was a Roman Catholic, an example followed by his friend Lord Arlington. Clifford the most honest of Charles's ministers, though he lacked flexibility, later resigned his office of Lord Treasurer because he could not take the Test Act. His conversion to Rome was a gradual process and was the result of much intellectual thought.

War was to be declared on the United Provinces by both Monarchs. They promised that neither would conclude a separate peace or truce with the Dutch without agreement of the other. It was King Louis's main responsibility to carry on the war by land, while King Charles promised to provide 6000 troops to be raised and maintained at his own expense. The English General would serve under the orders of the French Commander-in-Chief. The English negotiations had insisted that King Charles must be in charge of the war by sea. He was to provide 50 capital ships and 10 fireships, while Louis of France was to be responsible for 30 ships and 10 fireships. James Duke of York was to be appointed Commander-in-Chief by both Kings, and the French Vice-Admiral or Lieutenant-General was to serve directly under him. What most pleased Charles was the promised annual subsidy of 3,000,000 livres tournois (£200,000 for each year of the war with the Dutch), for he was always complaining that the Parliament's annual grant of £1,200,000 was insufficient for his needs. Parliament was too niggardly, so he now turned to Louis. With regard to the religious clause Charles wanted to please Minette and to a lesser degree Louis, but he was too much a political realist to believe that the English people would accept a Catholic king.

Charles was quite prepared to accept Louis's gold if his subjects should prove recalcitrant. One cannot defend his morality, but one can admire his cleverness. That does not mean that Charles and Madame were not right to seek a French alliance in 1670. Charles was a patriot in his insistence on the maintenance of Britain's sovereignty on the seas. The King and his sister had far more insight and political intelligence than the majority of their compatriots in regarding the Dutch as their enemies. Britain's role as an imperial power in the East and the New World owes much to Charles II, for her greatness was fostered during the bitter commercial and maritime wars with the Dutch.

Only two of Charles's Cabal, Clifford and Arlington, were in his confidence concerning the secret treaty. Buckingham was fooled, while Charles dared not trust Anthony Ashley Cooper, later Earl of Shaftesbury, a bitterly anti-Catholic protestant with the secret. 'Little Sincerity' as he nicknamed him, Lauderdale was a covenanter and at heart a persecutor. So soon as the treaty was signed Colbert de Croissy left for Boulogne where he handed his copy to King Louis. The ambassador was to write of Henriette D'Angleterre when he returned to Dover: 'It has seemed that Madame has more influence on her brother than any other person, not only by the eagerness that the ministers have shown in imploring her favour and support with the King.'⁵ Where others failed he was eager to grant her favours.

Now the business was concluded Madame was free to enjoy herself. It was her own birthday month of June, and since the weather remained beautiful, she and Charles took the opportunity of sailing in yachts along the Coast. On 8 June they paid a visit to the fleet. Members of her suite admired her courage. Like her brothers, she loved the sea. 'Madame is as bold as she is on land', wrote one of them, 'and walks as fearlessly along the edge of the ships as she does on shore.' What did brother and sister talk about on intimate occasions? Who can say? Of those distant days of exile when Charles was in love with 'Bablon'. Charles did not like her marrying a German Duke, she at least had the sense to insist that she would spend part of the year in France. Minette teased him, reminding Charles

171

of the time when 'Bablon' used to play the harpsichord for him in her yellow dress at Colombes. She refrained as much as possible to talk about her own unhappy marriage, and Charles respected her sensitivity.

One day Charles took his sister to Canterbury, where the actors of the Duke's House in London played Thomas Shadwell's *The Sullen Lovers*. It was based on Molière's *Les Facheux*, and the performance was intended to honour the King's sister. The Duke of Monmouth was so enchanted with the drollery of James Nokes in the part of Sir Arthur Addle, a Restoration fop, that he presented him with his sword. Queen Catherine was very uneasy when she saw her husband gazing too ardently at the baby-faced Bretonne Louise de Keroualle as she danced round a maypole. There was a collation in the hall of St. Augustine's Abbey.

The fugitive, precious days passed too quickly, and Charles was extremely generous to his sister, giving her 6000 pistoles towards her expenses, and 2000 gold crowns to build a chapel at Chaillot to commemorate their mother. He also gave her some precious jewels. By way of return Minette told Mademoiselle de Keroualle to fetch her jewel-casket, and asked her brother to choose any jewel that appealed to him. Taking the pretty Bretonne by the hand Charles declared that she was the only jewel he coveted and implored his sister to leave her behind in England. Slightly embarrassed, Minette explained that she was responsible to the girl's parents for their child, and had promised to bring her safely back to France.

When the Duchess of Orléans was about to leave England, Edmund Waller presented her with a poem:

That sun of Beauty did among us rise,
England first saw the light of your fair eyes;
in English too your early wit was shown;
Favour that language, which was then your own
When, though a child, through guards you made your way,
What fleet or army cou'd an angel stay?

Secret Diplomacy at Dover

Thrice happy Britain! If she cou'd retain
Whom she first lived within her ancient main....[6]

The King, the Duke of York and Prince Rupert accompanied Madame for some way on her journey to France. Slowly the Dover coast receded in the distance. The seagulls cried, swooping to the decks to pick up any morsels they could find. Charles could hardly bear to say goodbye to his sister, embracing her again and again, before he turned away. As her ship approached the coast of France, there was the thunder of great guns by way of royal salute welcoming Madame back to her adopted country.

XV

'Madame se meurt'

Madame landed at Calais, and with her retinue began her journey to Paris. King Louis, delighted by the success of his sister-in-law's mission, sent a detachment of his guards in her honour to Abbéville. From Abbéville she travelled to Beauvais where she was met by Ralph Montagu. If it had not been for Monsieur, Louis would himself have greeted Madame at Beauvais, but Monsieur showed his resentment against his wife by his absolute refusal to go.

His discourteous behaviour made it impossible for Louis and his Queen to meet her there. After much persuasion Monsieur agreed to meet his wife just outside St. Germain.

Madame received a joyful reception from the King and other members of the Royal Family, but Monsieur sulked, refusing his permission when his brother invited him and his wife to stay in Versailles. Though she appeared radiant and charming to the whole court, she was in reality extremely tired and unwell and was obliged to spend the day of her arrival in St. Germain in bed.

Louis was most generous, giving her a present of 6000 pistoles towards her expenses, assuring her that she could keep her brother's gift of the same amount for her own use. When she parted from the Queen and Mademoiselle, they both noticed she was in tears. The pleasure of her reception was marred by Monsieur's unkindness. He reminded her incessantly that since she had such great influence with the King, she could easily obtain permission from him for the Chevalier de Lorraine to be recalled. Madame knew this wasn't true.

Her prestige was at its height. When she reached Paris on

'Madame se Meurt'

20 June (New Style), foreign ambassadors hastened to pay their court, and to congratulate her on her return. All sorts of rumours were rampant, that she had managed to detach England from the Triple Alliance, and that a new alliance had sprung up between France and England. It was during the few days she spent in Paris that she found time to write to Sir Thomas Clifford, the only letter she ever attempted in English:

> When I have write to the King from Calais i praid him to tel milord Arlington an you what he had promised mi for bothe. his answer was that he gave mi againe his word, that he would performe the thing, but that hi did not thing it fit to exequte it now....
>
> This is the ferste letter I have ever write in inglis. you will eselay see it bi the stile and ortograf. prai see in the same time that I expose mi self to be thought a foulle in looking to make you know how much I am your frind.
>
> for Sir Thomas Clifort[1]

On 24 June Madame left for St. Cloud with her husband and her two daughters Marie-Louise and Anne-Marie, an infant of one year. It was a relief to Madame to leave for her beloved St. Cloud, for Paris was stifling in the sudden heat that had descended on France. It was a joy to Henriette D'Angleterre during this week of glorious sunshine to entertain her friends in her garden. Ralph Montagu the British Ambassador came to see her, accompanied by Lord Poulett and Sir Thomas Armstrong, two visiting Englishmen. Always she had loved music. Her guests were enchanted when she sang and played the guitar with all her old vivacity and charm. Monsieur did not care for music, although the second 'Madame' relates, that he would later spend the night of All Saints in Paris on purpose to hear the massed church-bells.[2] Madame now told Montagu about the secret treaty and that her brother and Louis intended to declare war on Holland.

Louis was anxious to see Madame to discuss the Treaty, and ordered his brother to bring his wife to Versailles for the day.

While they were engaged in a secret conference, Monsieur entered the room and was much incensed when they hurriedly broke off their conversation, refusing to continue it in his presence. At dinner that night a relation of Madame de Montespan's, M. de Tonnay-Charente, who had accompanied Madame to England, was tactless enough to infuriate Monsieur by harping on how attentive the Duke of Monmouth had been to his wife. The King rose from the table, observing that the young man must have been born in Madagascar.

Everybody agreed how ill poor Madame looked, and she left for St. Cloud only to be tormented by the nagging of her husband as their coach rattled along the highway. Some time during 26 June she sat down to write a last letter to Madame de St. Chaumont, telling her of her visit to her brother and how Monsieur incessantly found fault with her for the banishment of the Chevalier. Far from being all-powerful, Madame felt that his favourite's return depended little upon her. What was even more tragic was Madame's reference to her elder daughter, who was being taught to hate her. Her delicate health, ruined by the strain of the last few weeks, and in an overwrought state, she wrote bitterly to this intimate friend:

> I have often blamed you for the tender love you feel for my child. In God's name, put that love away. The poor child cannot return your affection, and will alas! be brought up to hate me ... you had better keep your love for persons who are as grateful as I am, and who feel as keenly as I do, the pain of being unable to help you in your present need.[3]

Madame has been accused of heartlessness when writing this letter, but she was a desperately unhappy woman. Monsieur and his minions were turning their child against her, and he often complained of the former royal governess to the King.

It was the season of strawberries and there they lay thick and luscious in the gardens. Madame was very fond of the fruit, but she now could hardly bear the sight of them. A fierce sun blazed down, and very unwisely against the advice of her doctor Yvelin* who had accompanied her to Dover, she bathed on the Friday in the Seine.

Afterwards she complained of sharp pains in her stomach. She needed the companionship of her devoted friend Marie-Madeleine de La Fayette, and invited her to St. Cloud. On Saturday evening 28 June Madame de La Fayette arrived and found the Princess in the gardens. The exquisite moonlight cast its magic on flower and tree, and sweet odours seemed to soothe Madame as she walked with her friend till a late hour.

Madame rose early on the Sunday morning and sat down to write a long letter to her cousin Anne de Gonzague, Princess Palantine, wife of Prince Edward, a younger son of Elizabeth of Bohemia.[4] Whilst Madame was in England, the Princess Palantine had asked her to persuade King Charles to pay her her pension. Nothing reveals more clearly how tormented Madame was about her marriage to Monsieur and of his relations with Lorraine. If fate had not struck her such a cruel blow, and if she had been spared a longer life, one wonders what was in store for her. Was not her early death when she had achieved her life-work indeed more merciful?

In her own words Madame de La Fayette described what happened on the Sunday morning.

She descended to Monsieur's apartments, who was bathing, and then visited me. She went to mass. On returning to her apartments, she leaned on me and said to me with that air of goodness, so characteristic of her that she would not be in such a bad humour if she could talk with me; but that she was so weary of all the people who surrounded her. She could not endure their presence.[5]

She went to see Marie-Lousie being painted by an English artist, and then talked in an animated way to her two friends Madame de La Fayette and Madame d'Epernon, who had just arrived, about her voyage to England and of the King her

* He sprang from an ancient Norman family, according to John Evelyn, who was related to him.

brother. It was the Princess's habit to lie down on cushions spread on the floor—'her head rested on my lap' relates Madame de La Fayette. She had already dined with her husband, and while Madame slept, Monsieur entertained the ladies. Marie-Madeleine felt a mounting uneasiness about her friend. As Princess Henriette slept, it seemed to her that a curious change had come to her face. Even Monsieur remarked how ill she looked as he prepared to leave for Paris. In the hall he ran into Madame de Meckelbourg—Henriette's intimate friend 'Bablon', eager no doubt to hear of her journey to England and of her brother Charles.

Madame asked for a glass of iced chicory water which was given her by one of her ladies, Madame de Gamaches, and handed to her by Madame de Gourdon. She was almost immediately seized with an agonizing pain in her side, and her first reaction was to cry out that she had been poisoned. Her ladies unlaced her dress and carried her to her bed. Once again she murmured that she had been poisoned. Marie-Madeleine looked keenly at Monsieur to detect any signs of guilt, but his behaviour was not that of a guilty man. He at once suggested that emetics should be given her and that a dog would be allowed to drink the chicory water. Meanwhile her devoted *femme de chambre* Madame des Bordes, who had served her all her life, drank some chicory water out of the same cup without any ill effects, as did 'Bablon', Madame de Meckelbourg, and even Monsieur, according to Bossuet's account later after her death to his brother. He drank from the same bottle. It was afterwards alleged that the Marquis d'Effiat, one of Monsieur's vile favourites had smeared the cup containing the chicory water with some poison received from the Chevalier de Lorraine in Rome. St. Simon, who was born five years after this tragic episode, repeats the story in his works. Although a fine writer, he is often prejudiced and embroidered the truth to suit his purposes. The later medical evidence is far more convincing that Madame died from natural causes.

All the same none of the doctors consulted, including

178

Madame's own doctor Yvelin, Esprit, and the King's doctor Vallot, diagnosed her illness correctly.

They were mistaken when they assured Monsieur that the Princess was in no danger. During the late seventeenth century the ignorance that prevailed among the medical confraternity was very marked. According to Madame de La Fayette, Madame alone insisted from the beginning that she was doomed to die, and despite her sufferings prepared to meet her end with her customary courage. To Monsieur she spoke with a sweetness, capable of melting the hardest heart, although she veiled her gentleness with a delicate reproach. 'Alas! Monsieur it is long since you have ceased to love me. That was unjust of you; I have never failed you.'[6] At this stage Monsieur seemed more bewildered than shocked at his wife's illness, but he was touched by his wife's words. A cup of broth only made her worse.

Meanwhile King Louis at Versailles had heard from the Duc de Crequi that, whatever the doctors might say, Madame was dying. He got into his coach together with the Queen, Madamoiselle de Montpensier and the Comtesse de Soissons once Madame's vindictive enemy. Louis was extremely agitated, for he was very fond of Madam. At about 11 p.m., he arrived at St. Cloud and at once hastened to Madame's bedside. A group of her friends were in the bedchamber, the old Maréchal de Gramont, father of the Comte de Guiche, who had loved her, the Maréchal de Turenne, Monsieur de Tréville, and the Prince de Condé. Together in a corner of the room were Madame de Montespan and the Duchesse de La Vallière once her maids-of-honour. Louis had no eyes for them now. Tears poured down his face as he implored the doctors to save Madame's life. Even the doctors were now convinced that she was a desperate case.

Mademoiselle wrote:

When we arrived at St. Cloud we found almost everybody afflicted. Monsieur seemed to be very bewildered. Madame

179

lay on a little bed with her nightdress unfastened and her
hair loose, her face was deadly pale; she had the air of a dead
person. Monsieur was saying to her: 'Madame, do your best
to vomit, so that this bile does not suffocate you.'

Madame embraced Louis and Marie-Thérèse, and spoke
kindly to both of them. To Mademoiselle, she said gently as
she pressed her hand: 'You are losing a good friend, who was
beginning to know and love you.' You can feel the sincerity
of the woman, her graciousness even in death, her charm as
she murmured to the King, who was far more distressed than
his brother: 'Ah, do not weep, Sire, or you will make me weep
too. You are losing a good servant who has always feared the
loss of your good graces more than death itself.' The King and
Queen left the bedchamber.

'*Madame se meurt.*' The awful words passed from mouth to
mouth. The King had told Monsieur to summon a priest, so
that Madame might receive the last comforts of her religion.
'Whose name will look best in the gazette?' asked Monsieur,
a question so characteristic of him that it almost staggers one.
Somebody suggested the Abbé Bossuet the magnificent
preacher, who had recently been appointed Bishop of Condom.
Monsieur was satisfied, and an urgent message was transmitted
to Bossuet to come at once. Meanwhile Madame de La Fayette
had already sent for Monsieur Feuillet, a Jansenist canon of
St. Cloud, an austere priest, fearless alike in his dealings both
with princes and more humble folk, yet he lacked Bossuet's
compassion and humanity. He told Madame to reflect on her
past life of selfish idulgence, her absorption in frivolous
pleasure. 'You have never known the true Christian faith,' he
told her. Madame now made a general confession to him. Even
the stern Jansenist priest was impressed by her courage and her
serenity, though she was in terrible pain.

There is a spirituality about her last hours on earth, deeply
moving for those who had loved her and now in anguish were
forced to watch her die. She had her faults, a hyper sensitivity

causing her occasionally to say an unkind word or to act too impulsively. She was a great soul, for she always inspired her friends to give of their best.

When Ralph Montagu, the British ambassador arrived, she prayed for strength, for she had much to say to him. Regarding the alliance with France and the war against Holland, she begged Montagu to tell her brother that she had only urged him to do this for his own honour and advantage. 'I have always loved my brother above all things in the world, and my only regret in dying is to leave him,' she told him. 'Madame,' Ralph Montagu suddenly said in English, 'Do you really believe that you have been poisoned?' Feuillet, alert and bristling, heard the word 'poison', very similar in French and severely told her that she must accuse nobody but offer up her life to God as a sacrifice. The Ambassador took no notice of the priest and repeated his question. Madame de Fayette heard her say in a low voice: 'Do not tell this to the King my brother; he must be spared that grief. Above all do not let him take vengeance on the King here, for he at least is not guilty.' She told Madame des Bordes in English to hand over to the Ambassador the casket containing the letters from her brother. It was imperative that they should not fall into the hands of others. Unfortunately her *femme de chambre* was so distressed by her mistress's imminent death that she had already given the casket to the Maréchal du Plessis on Monsieur's orders. At midnight Madame said goodbye to her husband for the last time, wishing now to think only of God.

The Abbé Bossuet at last entered the room, and Madame's poor, suffering face was transfigured with a gleam of joy. '*L'espérance, Madame, L'espérance,*' he said. The faithful few, who remained in the room, Madame de La Fayette, Madame d'Epernon, the distinguished scholar Monsieur de Tréville, who loved Madame, the Maréchal de Bellefonds, and Montagu sank to their knees. The Ambassador, too, had grown strongly attached to Madame. There was a nobility about him then in declining to accept the 6000 pistoles she offered him, saying

181

he would distribute it among her servants. Only later did his character coarsen.

The great bishop prayed with all the fervour possible for the soul of the beloved princess.

'Madame,' he said, 'you believe in God, you hope in God, you love god,' 'With all my heart,' she whispered, as the crucifix* she had clung to, fell from her hands. These were her last words.

* She told one of her maids to give Bossuet the emerald ring after her death.

Epilogue

When Charles II heard from Sir Thomas Armstrong the tragic news of his sister's death, he exclaimed vehemently: 'Monsieur is a villain! but Sir Thomas, I beg of you, not a word of this to others.' He confided to a friend, the Duc d'Elboeuf, 'my grief for her is so great, that I dare not allow myself to dwell upon it, and try so far as possible to think of other things'. All sorts of rumours were rampant in London that Madame had been poisoned. Colbert de Croissy told Lionne that the Duke of Buckingham had behaved like a madman, even urging at first that war should be declared on France. Very few people at Court really believed in the truth of the report. 'Prince Rupert, because he has a natural inclination to believe evil; the Duke of Buckingham, because he courts popularity, and Sir John Trevor, because he is Dutch at heart, and consequently hates the French.' Only King Charles and Lord Arlington behaved with good sense and moderation. It was vital that the alliance should continue.

It was absolutely essential for King Louis to order that a post-mortem examination of Madame's body should be held. There is an interesting contemporary translation of a letter from Lionne in the Record Office[1] showing that this took place on 30 June in the presence of about 100 people, including Ralph Montagu, the British Ambassador, Queen Catherine's own surgeons, and Dr. Hugh Chamberlain, an expert in feminine diseases. All the French doctors signed an official report that Madame's death was due to cholera morbus.[2] The English doctors also agreed that her death was owing to natural causes. Dr. Chamberlain and Alexander Boscher both seemed satisfied

183

Epilogue

at the time, but expressed some doubts afterwards that the surgeons had carried out the autopsy as if they wanted to conceal the truth. However, this may have been merely professional jealousy on the part of Chamberlain and Boscher.

All the medical evidence would show that Madame's health was very precarious throughout her brief life. As is well known, Charles was always imploring his sister to take good care of her health. The contemporary allusions by Gui Patin and Vallot prove that much anxiety was felt by many people for several years before her death. Lionne told the King that Madame had very often complained of 'a pricking in her side which forced her to ly downe 3 or 4 houres together on the ground finding no ease in any posture she placed herself in'.[3] Vallot's testimony was that for three or four years she lived as it were by miracle. In all his long experience he had never seen so much corruption as in Madame's body. That statement would be more convincing if he had at once taken her sudden illness seriously. Bossuet in his letter to his brother at Dijon wrote that Madame's stomach and heart were the only parts of her body to be found in good condition. These are usually the first organs to be attacked by poison.

Today most authorities agree that Madame's death was caused by acute peritonitis consequent upon the perforation of a duodenal ulcer. Dr. Jean Fabre in his scholarly work[4] discusses very seriously the problem whether Madame was poisoned. He came to the conclusion that the Princess died from natural causes. It is possible, however, that her death was due to porphyria,* a hereditary disease that has been traced back to her forebear Mary Queen of Scots. Porphyria may cause rapid death.[5] During the seventeenth century an unexplained death was sometimes conveniently attributed to foul play.

One thing is certain that there were evil, depraved people around Monsieur capable of committing such a vile act. St.

---

* A generalized disorder of which several types occur. They are characterized by purplish-coloured urine, abdominal symptoms and nervous mental derangements.

Epilogue

Simon's story that the Chevalier de Lorraine had sent a deadly poison from Rome to his accomplices the Marquis d'Effiat and the Comte de Beuvron is certainly very vivid.[6] He relates that during the afternoon of Sunday 29 June the Marquis D'Effiat was disturbed by a *garçon de la chambre* opening the cupboard of an antechamber in the palace of St. Cloud, and apparently assuaging his thirst with some water. The garçon sharply asked D'Effiat what he was doing, for nobody was authorized to open this cupboard. It contained Madame's chicory water. D'Effiat made some plausible excuse and there the matter rested for the present. Monsieur's second wife, Elisabeth Charlotte, Princess Palantine, always firmly believed that her predecessor had been poisoned, though absolutely convinced that it was done without the knowledge of her husband. He had not the temperament of a poisoner. He was such a tattler that he could never have kept the secret. Henriette D'Angleterre might think the Marquis d'Effiat less rascally than the Chevalier de Lorraine, but the second Madame was under no such illusions. She wrote of D'Effiat: 'To judge by his horrible vices and villainies, he must be already one of Lucifer's subjects.' 'There is no greater sodomite in the whole of France.'[7] She even feared in 1682 that she might meet the same fate as Henriette.

Ralph Montagu's opinion that Madame was poisoned—and he held it all his life (he died in 1709)—deserves more credit than Elisabeth Charlotte of Bavaria's belief, because he knew Madame well during the last year of her life. However, he may have been biased, for he disliked Monsieur and was devoted to the First Madame. It was natural for Montagu to criticize King Louis's decision to recall the Chevalier de Lorraine to court as a concession to Monsieur. This occurred during February 1672, just over a year and a half after Madame's death. He wrote to Arlington: 'If Madame were poisoned, as few people doubt, Lorraine is looked upon, by all France, to have done it ... and it is wondered at ... that this King should have so little regard to the King, our Master, considering how insolently he always carried himself to her when she was

185

Epilogue

alive. . . .' However, Lorraine's return really indicates that Louis believed that he was innocent, for otherwise he would hardly have agreed to it. The Marquis d'Effiat too, prospered with the years, and terminated his career as a member of the Regency Council under Louis XV. Charles himself was absolutely satisfied that Louis's conduct had been exemplary after his sister's death and that his grief showed his sincerity. It was a sagacious move on Louis's part to send over the Marechal de Bellefonds on an official mission of condolence to Charles, for he could give the King an account of the last scenes.

Colbert de Croissy informed Lionne that Charles had received Monsieur's envoy the Chevalier de Flamarins very coldly,[8] although this does not signify that he believed him guilty.

It was vital for Charles that all the letters he had written to his sister, particularly those concerning *the Grand Affaire* should be returned to him. Unfortunately, the letters were already in Monsieur's hands. Monsieur could not resist having read to him in French by one Carto, the husband of Madame's nurse, the letters written to his wife by the Duke of Monmouth. Louis told his brother to return them, and it is evident that much to Charles's relief they were handed over to him by the French ambassador on 7 July.* It seems likely that Charles destroyed some of the most confidential letters, for only five letters to his sister survive in the British museum. It is even possible that they once formed part of the collection at the Quai D'Orsay. Can one be certain even today that further correspondence between brother and sister may not be discovered?

Madame's vital part in the Treaty of Dover negotiations has been criticized, even condemned, particularly by historians of the last century, but she herself believed passionately that her advice to her brother and to Louis was right. Her magnetic personality made an enormous impression on her con-

* Cyril Hughes Hartmann thinks that Charles's ninety-eight letters now in the Quai D'Orsay were in another casket, and not discovered until afterwards.

temporaries. Her most intimate friends such as Madame de La Fayette, Monsieur de Tréville, the Maréchal de Turenne, and Daniel de Cosnac, Bishop of Valence (later Archbishop of Aix) never really recovered from the loss. 'This Great Princess', as Colbert de Croissy referred to her in his correspondence in the Quai D'Orsay, and she had an European reputation. In his letter of condolence to Charles II, Cardinal Barbarini wrote from his villa on the beautiful lake of Nemi near Rome: 'The rare qualities of this distinguished Princess were admired, not only by all France, but by the whole of Europe.' Yet she was only twenty-six when she died.

Notes

I 'BORN IN THE STORMS OF WAR', *pp. 5–14*

1 *The Worthies of England* by Dr Thomas Fuller, edited with an introduction and notes by John Freeman (1953).
2 J. B. Bossuet, *Oraison Funèbres* Préface de René Dominic.
3 Poems of Edmund Waller.
4 Calendar of State Papers, Charles II 1660–1670.

The title of the chapter is taken from Waller's poem to my Lady Morton on New Year's day, 1650, at the Louvre Palace. This poem, written in France, first appeared as a broadside, London-printed for Henry Heningman in the Lower Walk of the New Exchange 1661.

II EXILE IN FRANCE, *pp. 15–29*

1 *Mémoires de La Mission des Capuchins de La Province de Paris Près La Reine d'Angleterre Depuis L'Année 1630 Jusqu'a 1669.* Revus annôtes et publiés Par Le Apollenaire de Valence (1881).
2 p. 198 Mémoires de La Mission des Capuchins.
3 Nouvelle Biographe Générale Depuis Les Temps Les Plus Reculés Jusque Nos Jours par M. Firmin Didot Frères.
4 *Mémoires de Madame de Motteville* Sur Anne d'Autriche et sa Cour. Tome 2. p. 342.
5 *Mémoires de Cardinal de Retz.*
6 Nouvelle Collection des *Mémoires pour Servir a L'Historie de France.* Tome Quatrième. *Mémoires de Mme. de Montpensier.* Chéruel's edition.
7 Mademoiselle de Montpensier became later known as La Grande Mademoiselle owing to the fact that Monsieur Philippe d'Anjou after Gaston's death became duc d'Orléans and wished his eldest daughter to be called Mademoiselle. It was not owing to her excessive stature.
8 Copy of Charles II's letter Lambeth Palace Library. Codex Tenison 645.3.
9 *Historiettes by Tallemant des Reaux.*
10 *Prince Eugen of Savoy* by Nicholas Henderson (1964). See 3 (above) *Nouvelle Biographe Générale Depuis Les Temps Les Plus Reculés Jusque nos jours* par Mm. Firmin Didot Frères.
11 Marie-Madeleine Pioche de la Vergne Comtesse de la Fayette. Chaillot was formerly a 'pleasant house' belonging to the Marshal Bassompierre, according to the correspondence of Sir Richard Brown, resident at Paris.

Notes

III BROTHER AND SISTER, *pp. 30–36*

1 *The Memoirs of Sir John Reresby* (1875 edition), p. 42.
2 *The Tragedy of Charles II* by Hester Chapman (1964).
3 Letter at Ugbrooke Park among the Clifford Mss. Lord Clifford of Chudleigh kindly showed me a copy some years ago.
4 Codex Tenison 645.73. Lambeth Palace Library. The letter bears Princess Henriette's seal.
5 *Mémoires et Documents Politique Angleterre*, vol. 26, Quai D'Orsay, Paris.
6 *Mémoires et Documents Politique Angleterre*, vol. 26, Quai D'Orsay, Paris.
7 *Charles II and Madame* by Cyril Hughes Hartmann (1934).

IV MONSIEUR, *pp. 37–50*

1 *Monsieur Frère de Louis XIV* by Philippe Erlanger (1953).
2 Codex Tenison 645. Lambeth Palace Library.
3 Codex Tenison 645.119.
4 Treasury Books 1660–1667. Warrants of 9 November 1660 and 25 December 1661.
5 This street so full of historical interest bears the name of a local magistrate of the time of Henri IV, Princess Henriette's grandfather. In 1654 Catherine Bellier, known as One-Eyed Kate, first woman of the bedchamber to Anne of Austria had been ennobled and granted the site of the former town house of the abbots of Chaalis together with her husband Pierre Beauvais. During 1763 it was the property of the Bavarian Ambassador, and Mozart at the age of seven together with his parents stayed in this house.
6 *Mémoires de Père Cyprien de Gamaches.*
7 *Charles II* by Sir Arthur Bryant (1932).
8 *Memoirs and Correspondence of John Evelyn II.159* (edited from the original Mss. by William Bray).
9 *Diary and Correspondence of Samuel Pepys* with a Life and Notes by Richard Lord Braybrooke, vol. I, p. 125.
10 Correspondence Angleterre 74. M. Bartet to Cardinal Mazarin.
11 Commons Journals, 8, pp. 175 and 178. *Charles II and Madame* by Cyril Hughes Hartmann.
12 Correspondence Angleterre, Quai D'Orsay. Supplement 1660.
13 Charles II *Mémoires et Documents Politique Angleterre*, vol. 26, Quai D'Orsay No. 15.
14 *Histoire de Madame Henriette* by Madame de La Fayette.

Notes

V MADAME'S TRIUMPH, *pp. 51–63*

1 *Mémoires de Daniel de Cosnac archevêque d'aix Conseille du Roi en ses Conseils Commander de l'Ordre du Saint-Esprit* (1852). Tome Premier publiées pour le Societé de l'Histoire de France (1852). Tome Premier, p. 287.
2 Cosnac I, 287.
3 *Mémoires de L'Abbé de Choisy pour servir a L'Histoire de Louis XIV* Publiés avec Préface, Notes et Tables by M. de descure (1888), vol. ii.
4 *Louis XIV* by Vincent Cronin (1964). *Louis XIV* by Philippe Erlanger, translation (1970).
5 Julia Cartwright *Madame Henrietta Duchess of Orléans.* Also included in M. Anatole France's introduction to Madame de La Fayette's *Histoire de Madame Henriette.*
6 *Louis XIV* by Vincent Cronin.
7 *Mémoires de Madame de Motteville.*
8 *Louis XIV* by Vincent Cronin.
9 For Louise de La Vallière see Louise de La Vallière and the early life of Louis XIV from unpublished documents by Jules Lair.

VI INTRIGUES AND LOVE AFFAIRS, *pp. 64–76*

1 For De Guiche see W. H. Lewis *Assault on Olympus—a history of the De Gramont family*; also *Histoire de Madame Henriette* by Madame de La Fayette.
2 Codex Tenison 645,61. Lambeth Palace Library.
3 *Charles II and Madame* by Cyril Hughes Hartmann (1934).
4 C. H. 74 Ruvigni to Cardinal Mazarin, 17 October 1660.
5 Madame to Charles II, from Paris 4 January 1662. Cod. Tenison, 645,48.
6 See Bussy-Rabatin's *Histoires Amoureuse des Gaules.*
7 Codex Tenison 61.
8 S.P. France. Public Record Office 116.128. Endorsed *en faveur de Madame.* See also Charles II and Madame by Cyril Hughes Hartmann.
9 M. de Cominges' despatch, 27 October 1664. Correspondence Angleterre, 83 Quai D'Orsay.

VII FRUSTRATED NEGOTIATIONS, *pp. 77–93*

1 S.P. France. Public Record Office 116, f. 138.
2 Correspondence Angleterre, Louis XIV to Cominges.
3 *Mémoires et Documents Politique Angleterre*, vol. 26, Quai D'Orsay, No. 39.
4 Correspondence Angleterre 80, 26 October/5 November 1663.
5 See *History of His Own Time.* The History of the Reign of Charles II, p. 65 (1838 edition).
6 C.H. 80 Cominges to Louis XIV, 30 October 1663 (old Calendar).
7 S.P. France, 117, f. 192, Lord Holles to Charles II.

Notes

8 S.P. France, 117, Holles, 12/22 December 1663. Hartmann, Charles II and Madame.

9 S.P. France, 118, f. 261 Public Record Office. See also Holles's letter to Sir Henry Bennet, S.P. France, 118, f. 285. 29 June (old Calendar) 1664.

10 *Madame Henriette Duchess of Orléans* by Julia Cartwright.

11 Guy Patin, Lettres III.

12 Codex Tenison 645.60. 24 October 1664.

13 S.P. France, 130, f. 258. See also Cyril Hughes Hartmann, *Charles II and Madame*.

14 S.P. France, 119, f.157. Montpensier, IV. Mademoiselle's allusion to this incident corroborates Holles's letter.

VIII THE SECOND DUTCH WAR, *pp. 94–111*

1 *Louis XIV* by David Ogg (1967), p. 45.

2 Charles II. *Mémoires et Documents Angleterre*, vol. 26, Quai D'Orsay, vol. 26, Letter 61.

3 Ditto, Letter 76.

4 S.P. France, Record Office, 119, f. 218.

5 S.P. France, Record Office, 119, f. 228.

6 Codex Tenison 645.71.

7 Codex Tenison 645.49, 12 January 1664–5 (old Calendar).

8 *Mémoires*, Madame de La Fayette.

9 Letter Number 82, *Mémoires et Documents Angleterre*, vol. 26, January 1665.

10 *Charles II and Madame* by Cyril Hughes Hartmann.

11 See Keith Feiling's *British Foreign Policy 1660–1672*.

12 Codex Tenison 645.52.

13 S.P. France, 120.157.

14 Codex Tenison 645.53.

15 Codex Tenison 645.54.

16 C.A. 86, 16 July 1665. *Charles II and Madame*.

17 Codex Tenison 645.56.

18 *James II* by Jack Haswell (1972).

19 S.P. France, 120.153.

20 *Louis XIV* by David Ogg.

21 *Monsieur Frère de Louis XIV* by Philippe Erlanger (1953).

22 S.P. France, 119, f. 157.

23 S.P. France, 122, f. 155.

24 S.P. France, 122, f. 259.

Notes

IX PHILIPPE FALLS IN LOVE, *pp. 112–124*

1 *Mémoires de Daniel de Cosnac Archêveque d'Aix Conseiller du Roi en ses Conseils Commander de L'Ordre du Saint-Esprit.* Tome premier (1852 edition). Publiés par La Societé de L'Histoire de France.
2 *Charles II and Madame* by Cyril Hughes Hartmann.
3 *Mémoires* de Daniel de Cosnac.
4 *Mémoires* de Daniel de Cosnac, Tome I, p. 342.
5 *Mémoires* de Daniel de Cosnac, Tome I, p. 420.
6 *History of His Own Time.* The History of the Reign of Charles II, p. 201 (1838 edition).
7 *Mémoires et Documents Angleterre Politique*, vol. 26.
8 *Mémoires* de L'Abbé de Choisy, p. 70.
9 *Mémoires* de Daniel de Cosnac.

X MADAMES INTEREST IN LITERATURE AND DRAMA, *pp. 125–130*

1 *Molière. His Life and Works* by John Palmer (1930).
2 Jean Racine. *A critical biography by Geoffrey Brereton* (1951).
3 Les lettres de Messire Roger de Rabutin Comte de Bussy. Lieutenant General des Armées du Roi, et Mastre de Camp general de La Cavalerie Française et Etrangère. Tome Troisiemè.
4 *History of His Own Time.*
5 Daughter of Madame's younger daughter Anne-Marie, born 1669. In 1684 she married Victor Amadeus II, Duke of Savoy. Lucy Norton in her recent biography *First Lady of Versailles* (1977) reveals that Marie Adélaïde as Dauphone of France developed a more serious side to her character.

XI PRELIMINARY NEGOTIATIONS, *pp. 131–139*

1 See *Life, Works and Correspondence of Sir William Temple* by Sir Peregrine Courtenay (2 vols, 1836).
2 Quai D'Orsay Mémoires et Documents Politique Angleterre, vol. 26, Letter 116.
3 Hist. Mss. Commission Duke of Buccleuch (1899), R. Montagu to Lord Arlington.
4 *Mémoires de L'Abbe de Choisy*, vol. II p. 62.
5 C.A. 97.

XII 'THE GREAT SECRET', *pp. 140–151*

1 *King Charles II* by Sir Arthur Bryant.
2 S.P. France, 126. f. 124.
3 S.P. France, 126. f. 156.

Notes

4 C.A. 93. Lionne to Colbert de Croissy, February 1669.
5 Correspondence Angleterre 94, f. 333. Colbert de Croissy to Lionne.
6 A copy of Madame's letter of February 1669 can be studied in the Quai D'Orsay, C.A. 93, f. 240. Contained in a despatch from Lionne to Colbert de Croissy.
7 C.A., 92, f. 6. Original in French. Letter written in July 1669.
8 Mémoires et Documents Politique Angleterre, vol. 26, No. 150.
9 Hist. Mss. Comm. Duke of Buccleuch R. Montagu to Lady Harvey 26 August 1669.
10 *Charles II and Madame* by Cyril Hughes Hartmann.
11 Clifford Mss.
12 *The Handle and the Axe* by J. H. Aveling.
13 *Oraison Funèbres*, Préface de Rene Doumic.
14 *The Life of Queen Henrietta Maria*, vol. II by J. A. Taylor.
15 *Louis XIV* by David Ogg (1967); paperback edition.
16 Keith Feiling (later Sir Keith) suggests this in his interesting article in the English Historical Review, vol. 43, pp. 396–7 in which he gives an English translation of Madame's letter.
17 This letter in the original French is amongst the Clifford Mss. at Ugbrooke Park. It was written on 29 September 1669 at St. Cloud.
18 *The Handle and the Axe* by J. C. H. Aveling (1976).
19 *Charles II and Madame* by Cyril Hughes Hartmann.
20 Clifford Mss. Colbert de Croissy's commission to treat. Dated 21–31 October, 1669. Copy in Sir Richard Belling's handwriting.

XIII MADAME'S DOMESTIC TROUBLES, *pp. 152–163*

1 The letter is included in Cosnac, *Mémoires*, vol. I.
2 Lettre de Madame, 28 December 1669, Cosnac, *Mémoires*, I.
3 Hist. Mss. Comm. Duke of Buccleuch (1899).
4 Correspondence Angleterre 97, 2 January 1670.
5 *Mémoires de Mademoiselle de Montpensier.*
6 See *Mémoires de Mademoiselle de Montpensier.* Madame said: 'J'ai une peine mortelle de celle de Monsieur.'
7 Hist. Mss. Commission Duke of Buccleuch I (1899). R. Montagu to Arlington, 1 February 1670.
8 Julia Cartwright, *Madame Henriette Duchess of Orléans.*
9 Clifford Mss. Endorsed 'Sent to Madam January 24 69/70. To be translated by Mr. Montagu, *not* Ralph Montagu the ambassador.
10 *Charles II and Madame* by Cyril Hughes Hartmann.
11 S.P. France, 129.44.
12 S.P. France, Old Calendar Style, 14–24 February 1670.
13 C.A. 97.

Notes

14 *Charles II and Madame* by Cyril Hughes Hartmann.
15 16 April 1670.

XIV SECRET DIPLOMACY AT DOVER, *pp. 164–173*

1 La Grande Mademoiselle wrote an interesting account of the journey, while Pellisson was the official chronicler.
2 William Perwich to Sir Joseph Williamson, Secretary of State. Sidney Godolphin bore the letter.
3 Erlanger. Monsieur Frère de Louis XIV.
4 Correspondence Angleterre 97.
5 Correspondence Angleterre Politique 97, f. 33.
6 Edmund Waller Poems (1912). Poems written upon several occasions by Edmund Waller. To the Duchess of Orléans when she was taking leave of the Court at Dover in the year 1670.

XV 'MADAME SE MEURT' *pp. 174–182*

1 This quaint letter is among the Clifford Mss. at Ugbrooke Park. First printed by Keith Feiling in the English Historical Review, vol. 143. Charles II did not forget his promise, although he delayed creating Arlington an Earl until April 1672 and Clifford a peer on the same date, mainly because it was essential for the Treaty of Dover to be kept a secret.
2 Letters from Liselotte. Elisabeth Charlotte, Princess Palatine and Duchess of Orléans 'Madame' 1652–1722. Translated and edited by Marie Kroll (1970).
3 Cartwright. *Madame Henrietta Duchess of Orléans*. Marie-Louise married Charles II of Spain and died like her mother in mysterious circumstances aged twenty-six.
4 This is the last letter Madame ever wrote. Formerly it was questioned whether it was authentic, now it is certainly considered hers. There is a copy in French at Ugbrooke Park, endorsed in Sir Thomas Clifford's hand 'Madam's L from St. Cloud,' It has been translated by Mr. Hartmann ('Charles II and Madame'). Ralph Montagu's letter to Arlington from Paris 1 August 1670 proves that Madame did write to the Princess Palatine on 29 June 1670.
5 *Histoire de Madame Henriette D'Angleterre.*
6 Madame de La Fayette was an eye-witness throughout the last scenes up to Madame's death. Her account is probably the best, but other sources are Mademoiselle de Montpensier's Memoires, Ralph Montagu's letters to Arlington and Charles II, Perwich S.P. France, 129, and Bossuet's letter to his brother.

195

Notes

EPILOGUE *pp. 183–187*

1 S.P. France, 129, f. 283.
2 S.P. France, 129, f. 280.
3 S.P. France, 129, f. 283.
4 *Sur la Vie et Principalement sur la mort de Madame Henriette-Anne Stuart Duchesse d'Orléans (1912)* by Dr. Jean Fabre.
5 *Tenements of Clay.* An Anthology of Medical biographical essays (chosen and edited by Arthur Sorsby, 1974).
6 *Mémoires de Saint-Simon 8.* Nouvelle Edition Par A. Buislisle (Paris 1891), p. 375.
7 Letters from Liselotte. Elisabeth Charlotte and Duchesse D'Orléans (1970). To her favourite Stepbrother known as Carlluz (Versailles, 23 August 1682).
8 C.A. 98. Colbert de Croissy to Colbert, 7 July 1670.

Bibliography of
Princess Henrietta-Anne
Duchess of Orleans

PRIMARY SOURCES

Manuscript material.
Twenty-three of Madame's letters in the Lambeth Palace Library. Codex Tenison, 645. Eight of Madame's letters in the Record Office, Chancery Lane.

S.P. Foreign: France, 116, f. 128.

S.P. Foreign: France, 116, f. 138.

S.P. France: 117, f. 198.

S.P. France: 118, f. 261.

S.P. France: 119, f. 218.

S.P. France: 122, f. 9.

S.P. France: 119, f. 176.

S.P. France 116, f. 133.

Five letters of Charles II to his sister: Mss. British Museum.

Three of Madame's letters at Ugbrooke Park, Devon among the Clifford Mss. One in English to Sir Thomas Clifford; one in French to Lord Arlington; one in French to Charles II (dated 29 September 1669).

Ninety-eight of Charles II's letters preserved at the Quai D'Orsay.

Mémoires et Documents Angleterre Politique, vol. 26.

Perwich's despatches among the State Papers, Foreign Record Office. Also published by the Camden Society.

Correspondence Politique: Angleterre.

Correspondence of French Ambassadors at Court of St. James's. C.A. 74–98.

Correspondence of Denzil Lord Holles, British Ambassador in France, Letter to Charles II and Sir Henry Bennet (later Lord Arlington) (unpublished), S.P. France, 117, etc.

Bibliography

Correspondence of Ralph Montagu, British Ambassador in France. Letters to Lord Arlington and Charles II (unpublished), S.P. France, 126, etc.

The Secret Treaty of Dover papers among the Clifford Mss., of extreme importance.

Five of Charles II's letters in the British Museum. Additional Ms, 18, 738, f. 108 and other manuscripts.

Also, additional Ms, 18, 738, f. 102.

Historical Mss Commission Duke of Buccleuch I (1899).

Ralph Montagu to Lord Arlington. These letters are published.

PREVIOUS BOOKS ABOUT PRINCESS HENRIETTA-ANNE DUCHESS OF ORLÉANS

Madame. A Life of Henrietta, daughter of Charles I and Duchess of Orleans (*1894*) by Julia Cartwright (Mrs. Henry Ady).

Charles II and Madame by Cyril Hughes Hartmann (1934).

Henriette Anne d'Angleterre, Duchesse d'Orléans, sa vie et sa correspondance avec son frère Charles II, 1886 by Comte de Baillon.

Lives of the Four Last Stuart Princesses, by Agnes Strickland.

Historie de Madame Henriette d'Angleterre (a contemporary work, important) by Madame de La Fayette.

Lives of the Princesses of England by Mrs. Everett-Green.

Sur La Vie et Principalement sur la mort de Madame, Henriette-Anne Stuart, Duchesse d'Orléans, 1912 by Dr. Jean Fabre.

Oraisons Funèbres Préface de René Doumic by J. B. Bossuet (Particularly Oraison Funèbre de La Reine de La Grande-Bretagne and Oraison Funèbre de Henriette d'Angleterre).

Royal Flush. The Story of Minette by Margaret Irwin (1932). Vivid account of her life, but *not* a biography.

CONTEMPORARY WORKS

Mémoires de Duc de Saint-Simon 8. Nouvelle Edition Par A. Boislisle (Paris 1891).

Mémoires de Madame de Motteville Sur Anne D'Autriche et sa Cour, particularly Tomes 2 and 4.

Nouvelle Collection des Mémoires pour servir a L'Histoire de France. Tome Quatrième. *Mademoiselle de Montpensier.*

Mémoires de L'Abbé de Choisy pour servir a L'Histoire de Louis XIV publiés avec Préface, Notes et Tables by Monsieur de Lescure (1888). Vols I and II.

Bibliography

Mémoires de Daniel de Cosnac Archevêque d'Aix Conseiller du Roi en ses conseils Commandeur de L'Ordre du Saint-Esprit. Publiés pour la Societé de L'Histoire de France (1852). Tomes I and II.

Guy Patin's letters.

Diary and Correspondence of Samuel Pepys with a Life and note by Richard Lord Braybrooke, vol. I (1894).

Memoirs of the Count de Grammont by Count Anthony Hamilton (1928 edition). Translated by Horace Walpole.

Memoirs of John Evelyn edited from the original Mss, by William Bray, vol. II, (1827).

Les Lettres de Messire Roger de Rabutin Comte de Bussy. Lieutenant General Des Armées de Roi, etc. Tome Troisiéme.

History of His Own Time. The History of the Reign of Charles II by Bishop Gilbert Burnet (1838 edition).

The Worthies of England bt Dr. Thomas Fuller (edited and introduction and notes by John Freeman 1953).

The Memoirs of Sir John Reresby of Thrybergh, Bart. M.P. for York. edited from the original manuscript by James Cartwright, M.A.

The Mémoires of Cardinal de Retz (1875).

Mémoires de La Mission des Capuchins de La Province de Paris Pres La Reine d'Angleterre Depuis L'Anneé 1630 Jusqu'a 1669. Père Cyprien de Gamaches is a good source for early life of Princess Henrietta.

OTHER WORKS CONSULTED

The Escape of Charles II by Richard Ollard (1966).

Charles II by Sir Arthur Bryant (1931).

The Tragedy of Charles II in the years 1630–1660 by Hester Chapman (1964).

Charles II. His Life and Likeness (1960) by Hesketh Pearson.

The Stuarts by J. B. Kenyon (1958).

Louis XIV by Vincent Cronin (1964).

Louis XIV by Philippe Erlanger (1970).

Monsieur Frére de Louis XIV by Philippe Erlanger (1953).

Louis XIV by David Ogg (reprinted as a paperback 1973).

Clifford of the Cabal. A Life of Thomas, First Lord Clifford of Chudleigh by Cyril Hughes Hartmann (1937).

Prince Eugen of Savoy by Nicholas Henderson (1964).

The Life of Queen Henrietta Maria by L. A. Taylor. Vols I and II (1905).

The Life, Works and Correspondence of Sir William Temple by Sir Peregrine Courtenay (2 vols, 1836).

The Handle and the Axe by J. C. H. Aveling.

The Letters of Elizabeth Queen of Bohemia compiled by L. M. Baker (1953).

Bibliography

Assault on Olympus, a history of the De Grammont family by W. H. Lewis (1976).

Jean Racine: a Critical Biography by Geoffrey Brereton (1951).

Molière: His Life and Works by John Palmer (1930).

James Duke of Monmouth by Bryan Bevan (1973).

The Protestant Duke. A Life of the Duke of Monmouth by Violet Wynham (1976).

James Duke of Monmouth by Elizabeth D'Oyley (1938).

Louise de La Vallière and the Early Life of Louis XIV from unpublished documents by Jules Lair. Translated from the Fourth French edition by Ethel Colturn Mayne.

Keith Feiling. Article in English Historical Review, vol. 43, pp. 396–7.

James II by Jock Haswell (1972).

British Foreign Policy 1660–1672 by Keith Feiling.

The Stuarts in Love by Maurice Ashley (1963).

Charles II, The Man and the Statesman by Maurice Ashley (1971).

Daughter of France. The Life of Anne Marie Louise D'Orléans Duchesse de Montpensier 1627–1693 by V. Sackville-West (1959).

England under the Stuarts by G. M. Trevelyan (first published 1904).

Etudes sur La Vie de Jacques Bossuet (Natus 27 September 1627), Jusqu'a son entrée en fonctions en Qualité de Pecepteur du Dauphin Par H. Floquet (Paris 1855).

See also Lettre Inédite de Bossuet sur la mort d'Henriette-Anne D'Angleterre Duchesse d'Orléans 8° Ln.[27], 42507. 1855 by A. Floquet. 30 Juin, 1670. Bibliothèque Nationale.

Index

Index

Index

Index

Index

Index